Timeless Quotations on

FAITH & BELIEF

Timeless Quotations on

FAITH

&

BELIEF

Compiled by John Cook

Fairview Press
Minneapolis

Published by Fairview Press, 2450 Riverside Avenue South, Minneapolis, MN 55454.

Library of Congress Cataloging-in-Publication Data
Timeless quotations on faith & belief / compiled by
    John Cook.
        p.   cm. -- (Pocket positives)
    ISBN 1-57749-060-6 (alk. paper)
    1. Spiritual life--Quotations, maxims, etc.
    I. Cook, John, 1939–   . II. Series.
    BL624.T55   1997
    291'.4--dc21   97-31319
                                                    CIP

First Printing: November 1997
Printed in the United States of America
01 00 99 98 97   7 6 5 4 3 2 1

Cover design: Laurie Duren

Publisher's Note: The publications of Fairview Press, including the Pocket Positives™ series, do not necessarily reflect the philosophy of Fairview Health System or its treatment programs.

For a free catalogue, call toll-free 1–800–544–8207. Visit our web site at www.press.Fairview.org.

for Freddi, Blake, Brian, and Timmy

CONTENTS

INTRODUCTION

THE BOOKS IN THE POCKET POSITIVES™ SERIES
originated as a selection of life-affirming
quotations I compiled for my nephews
and niece for Christmas 1989.

Because I was concerned that one of
them was too young for it, I wrote in a
letter that accompanied the collection,
"just put it away in a safe place until
you're ready for it." To address the question of how someone would know they
were "ready," I wrote:

"You'll be ready the first time things
don't go the way you want them to, the
first time you doubt your ability to do
something, the first time you're tempted
to quit or give up, the first time you
actually fail at something.

"You'll be ready the first time you
doubt a friend, or think you can't trust
anyone.

"You'll be ready the first time you have
to make an important decision, or choice.

"You'll be ready the first time you're afraid of something, or worried.

"You'll know when you're ready. When you are, these thoughts should give you the courage and confidence and spirit you need … and they'll remind you of the wonder and the joy of life, regardless of how dark things seem at the moment.

"I know they will…. They always have for me."

So, in addition to being a resource for researchers, writers, students, and professionals, I hope this book—and all the books in the Pocket Positives™ series—will provide comfort and inspiration for the casual browser or reader.

• • •

Numerous questions and concerns about accuracy confront anyone who compiles quotations. Take, for example, differences in the spelling of sources' names. The same famous Russian novelist has had his name spelled "Dostoevski," "Dostoievski," and "Dostoyevsky."

The formality required to identify sources is another issue. The Spanish Jesuit writer Baltasar Gracian Y Morales, for example, is more commonly referred to as "Baltasar Gracian," or simply "Gracian." And some sources are almost universally referred to by only one name, usually in the interest of brevity, and because it would be difficult to confuse them with anyone else. "Crebillion," for example, is used for Prosper Jolyot de Crebillion, the French dramatic poet.

And, of course, through the years many exact quotations—and even more that are very similar—have been attributed to more than one source.

I have made every effort to present each quotation as accurately as possible, and to recognize and honor the appropriate source. In particularly demanding situations, the language and sources cited are those most often used by other compilers and editors. Where it was impossible to verify the accuracy or source of a quotation, I have included it anyway if I believed that the usefulness of the quotation outweighed the demands of scholarly rigor.

PART ONE

OUR HIGHER POWER

We Can't, Don't Need, and Aren't Expected to Understand God

It is the heart which experiences God, not the reason.

—Blaise Pascal

I believe in the incomprehensibility of God.

—Honore de Balzac

Every conjecture we can form with regard to the works of God has as little probability as the conjectures of a child with regard to the works of a man.

—Thomas Reid

No statement about God is simply, literally true. God is far more than can be measured, described, defined in ordinary language, or pinned down to any particular happening.

—David Jenkins

Who fathoms the Eternal Thought?
Who talks of scheme and plan?
The Lord is God! He needeth not
The poor device of man.
                    —John Greenleaf Whittier

Some people want to see God with their
eyes as they see a cow, and to love Him
as they love their cow—for the milk and
cheese and profit it brings them. This is
how it is with people who love God for
the sake of outward wealth or inward
comfort.
                    —Meister Eckhart

Your mind cannot possibly understand
God. Your heart already knows. Minds
were designed for carrying out the orders
of the heart.
                    —Emmanuel

A comprehended God is no God at all.
                    —Gerhard Tersteegen

"What do you think of God," the teacher asked. After a pause, the young pupil replied, "He's not a think, he's a feel."
—Paul Frost

There is but one ultimate Power. This Power is to each one what he is to it.
—Ernest Holmes

God, to be God, must transcend what is. He must be the maker of what ought to be.
—Rufus M. Jones

To them that ask, where have you seen the Gods, or how do you know for certain there are Gods, that you are so devout in their worship? I answer: Neither have I ever seen my own soul, and yet I respect and honor it.
—Marcus Aurelius

God is an unutterable sigh, planted in the depths of the soul.
—Jean Paul Richter

GOD MAY BE DIFFERENT
TO EACH OF US

God is like a mirror. The mirror never
changes, but everybody who looks at it
sees something different.
                    —Rabbi Harold Kushner

God is to me that creative Force, behind
and in the universe, who manifests
Himself as energy, as life, as order, as
beauty, as thought, as conscience, as love.
                    —Henry Sloane Coffin

God is incorporeal, divine, supreme, infinite. Mind, Spirit, Soul, Principle, Life,
Truth, Love.
                    —Mary Baker Eddy

The God of many men is little more
than their court of appeal against the
damnatory judgement passed on their
failures by the opinion of the world.
                    —William James

God is a verb, not a noun.

—R. Buckminster Fuller

The most beautiful of all emblems is that of God, whom Timaeus of Locris describes under the image of "A circle whose centre is everywhere and whose circumference is nowhere."

—Voltaire

God has many names, though He is only one Being.

—Aristotle

God is what man finds that is divine in himself. God is the best way man can behave in the ordinary occasions of life, and the farthest point to which man can stretch himself.

—Max Lerner

God, that dumping ground of our dreams.

—Jean Rostand

6

HOW TO FIND AND REACH GOD

When we lose God, it is not God who is lost.

> —Anon.

God enters by a private door into every individual.

> —Ralph Waldo Emerson

A humble knowledge of oneself is a surer road to God than a deep searching of the sciences.

> —Thomas a'Kempis

By learning to contact, listen to, and act on our intuition, we can directly connect to the higher power of the universe and allow it to become our guiding force.

> —Shakti Gawain

In the faces of men and women I see God.

> —Walt Whitman

Some people talk about finding God, as
if He could get lost.

—Anon.

All who call on God in true faith,
earnestly from the heart, will certainly be
heard, and will receive what they have
asked and desired.

—Martin Luther

Hunting God is a great adventure.

—Marie DeFloris

To Be is to live with God.

—Ralph Waldo Emerson

Nothing hath separated us from God but
our own will, or rather our own will is
our separation from God.

—William Law

The kingdom of God is within you.

—Lk. 17:21

Not only then has each man his individual relation to God, but each man has his peculiar relation to God.

—George MacDonald

Because you cannot see him, God is everywhere.

—Yasunari Kawabata

It's only by forgetting yourself that you draw near to God.

—Henry David Thoreau

The light of God surrounds me,
The love of God enfolds me,
The power of God protects me,
The Presence of God watches over me,
Wherever I am, God is.

—Prayer Card

To think you are separate from God is to remain separate from your own being.

—D.M. Street

GOD WILL HELP US

Without the assistance of the Divine
Being ... I cannot succeed. With that
assistance, I cannot fail.
                                        —Abraham Lincoln

Whoever falls from God's right hand Is
caught into His left.
                                        —Edwin Markham

Pardon, not wrath, is God's best
attribute.
                                        —Bayard Taylor

In God We Trust.
                    —Motto of the United States,
                        adopted by Congress for use
                        on coins and one-dollar bills

I will not fear, for you are ever with me,
and you will never leave me to face my
perils alone.
                                        —Thomas Merton

Walk boldly and wisely.... There is a
hand above that will help you on.
—Philip James Bailey

The things which are impossible with
men are possible with God.
—Lk. 18:27

Whom the heart of man shuts out,
Sometimes the heart of God takes in.
—James Russell Lowell

For the multitude of worldly friends
profiteth not, nor may strong helpers
anything avail, nor wise counselors give
profitable counsel, nor the cunning of
doctors give consolation, nor riches
deliver in time of need, nor a secret
place to defend, if Thou, Lord, do not
assist, help, comfort, counsel, inform,
and defend.
—Thomas a'Kempis

Some Ways That God Makes Wishes Known to Us

Trust in the Lord with all thine heart, and lean not unto thine own understanding. In all thy ways acknowledge Him, and He shall direct thy paths.

—Prv. 3:5–6

God speaks to all individuals through what happens to them moment by moment.

—J.P. DeCaussade

God uses lust to impel men to marry, ambition to office, avarice to earning, and fear to faith. God led me like an old blind goat.

—Martin Luther

An act of God was defined as "something which no reasonable man could have expected."

—A.P. Herbert

GOD AND LOVE

Let God love you through others and let
God love others through you.
                                    —D.M. Street

One unquestioned text we read,
All doubt beyond, all fear above;
Nor crackling pile nor cursing creed
Can burn or blot it: God is Love.
                          —Oliver Wendell Holmes

A true love of God must begin with a
delight in his holiness.
                              —Jonathan Edwards

No man hates God without first hating
himself.
                                —Fulton J. Sheen

Don't try to reach God with your understanding; that is impossible. Reach him
in love; that is possible.
                               —Carlo Carretto

General Quotations about a Higher Power, or God

I have never understood why it should be considered derogatory to the Creator to suppose that He has a sense of humor.

—William Ralph Inge

"You are accepted!" ... accepted by that which is greater than you and the name of which you do not know. Do not ask the name now, perhaps you will know it later. Do not try to do anything, perhaps later you will do much. Do not seek for anything, do not perform anything, do not intend anything. Simply accept the fact that you are accepted.

—Paul Tillich

Every law of matter or the body, supposed to govern man, is rendered null and void by the law of Life, God.

—Mary Baker Eddy

God knows no distance.

—Charleszetta Waddles

The deep emotional conviction of the
presence of a superior reasoning power,
which is revealed in the incomprehensi-
ble universe, forms my idea of God.

—Albert Einstein

I would rather walk with God in the
dark than go alone in the light.

—Mary Gardiner Brainard

What we are is God's gift to us. What we
become is our gift to God.

—Anon.

God delays, but doesn't forget.

—Spanish proverb

How is it, Lord, that we are cowards in
everything save in opposing Thee?

—Saint Teresa of Avila

God is clever, but not dishonest.

—Albert Einstein

Above all am I convinced of the need, irrevocable and inescapable, of every human heart, for God. No matter how we try to escape, to lose ourselves in restless seeking, we cannot separate ourselves from our divine source. There is no substitute for God.

—A.J. Cronin

Gawd knows, and 'E won't split on a pal.

—Rudyard Kipling

What is there in man so worthy of honor and reverence as this, that he is capable of contemplating something higher than his own reason, more sublime than the whole universe—that Spirit which alone is self-subsistent, from which all truth proceeds, without which there is no truth?

—Friedrich Jacobi

God is no enemy to you. He asks no more than that He hear you call Him "Friend."

—*A Course in Miracles*

Yet, in the maddening maze of things,
And tossed by storm and flood,
To one fixed trust my spirit clings;
I know that God is good!

—John Greenleaf Whittier

A consciousness of God releases the greatest power of all.

—*Science of Mind*

Talking about God is not at all the same thing as experiencing God, or acting out God through our lives.

—Phillip Hewett

Courage is not afraid to weep, and she is not afraid to pray, even when she is not sure who she is praying to.

—J. Ruth Gendler

The person who has a firm trust in
the Supreme Being is powerful in his
power, wise by his wisdom, happy by
his happiness.

—Joseph Addison

Our human resources, as marshalled by
the will, were not sufficient; they failed
utterly.... Every day is a day when we
must carry the vision of God's will into
all our activities.

—Alcoholics Anonymous

God has not promised skies always blue,
flower-strewn pathways all our lives
   through;
God has not promised sun without rain,
joy without sorrow, peace without pain.
But God has promised strength for the
   day,
rest for the labor, light for the way,
Grace for the trials, help from above,
unfailing sympathy, undying love.

—Kristone

Every morning I spend fifteen minutes
filling my mind full of God, and so
there's no room left for worry thoughts.
                    —Howard Chandler Christy

Darkness is strong, and so is Sin,
But surely God endures forever!
                    —James Russell Lowell

We have grasped the mystery of the atom
and rejected the Sermon on the Mount.
                    —General Omar N. Bradley

Deep down in every man, woman and
child, is the fundamental idea of God. It
may be obscured by calamity, by pomp,
by worship of other things, but in some
form or other it is there. For faith in a
Power greater than ourselves, and mirac-
ulous demonstrations of that power in
human lives, are facts as old as man
himself.
                    —Alcoholics Anonymous

Then comes the insight that All is God. One still realizes that the world is as it was, but it does not matter, it does not affect one's faith.

—Abraham Heschel

The experience of God, or in any case the possibility of experiencing God, is innate.

—Alice Walker

Before me, even as behind, God is, and all is well.

—John Greenleaf Whittier

Forgetfulness of self is remembrance of God.

—Bayazid Al-Bistami

PART TWO

FAITH & BELIEF

WE MUST HAVE FAITH
IN WHAT WE CAN'T SEE

I believe in the sun even if it isn't shining. I believe in love even when I am alone. I believe in God even when He is silent.

—World War II refugee

Faith is the daring of the soul to go farther than it can see.

—William Newton Clark

Faith is the substance of things hoped for, the evidence of things not seen.

—Heb. 11:1

All I have seen teaches me to trust the Creator for all I have not seen.

—Ralph Waldo Emerson

Some things have to be believed to be seen.

—Ralph Hodgson

Faith is like radar that sees through the fog—the reality of things at a distance that the human eye cannot see.

—Corrie Ten Boom

You have to believe in gods to see them.

—Hopi Indian saying

Faith declares what the senses do not see, but not the contrary of what they see.

—Blaise Pascal

Faith sees the invisible, believes the incredible and receives the impossible.

—Anon.

A believer, a mind whose faith is consciousness, is never disturbed because other persons do not yet see the fact which he sees.

—Ralph Waldo Emerson

We walk by faith, not by sight.

—2 Cor. 5:7

Faith is to believe what we do not see;
the reward of this faith is to see what we
believe.

—Saint Augustine

Because you cannot see him, God is
everywhere.

—Yasunari Kawabata

Sorrow looks back, worry looks around,
faith looks up.

—*Guideposts*

Faith has to do with things that are not
seen, and hope with things that are not
in hand.

—Saint Thomas Aquinas

Faith is the capacity of the soul to perceive the abiding ... the invisible in the
visible.

—Leo Baeck

WE MUST HAVE FAITH
IN OTHER PEOPLE

We must have infinite faith in each other.
—Henry David Thoreau

Faith in our associates is part of our faith in God.
—Charles Horton Cooley

Faith enables persons to be persons because it lets God be God.
—Carter Lindberg

He who has no faith in others shall find no faith in them.
—Lao-tzu

Don't lose faith in humanity: think of all the people in the United States who have never played you a single nasty trick.
—Elbert Hubbard

WE MUST HAVE FAITH
IN OURSELVES

Only the person who has faith in himself
is able to be faithful to others.
—Erich Fromm

Faith, as an intellectual state, is self-
reliance.
—Oliver Wendell Holmes

Faith consists, not in ignorance, but in
knowledge, and that, not only of God,
but also of the divine will.
—John Calvin

Faith in oneself ... is the best and safest
course.
—Michelangelo

Faith is an attitude of the person. It
means you are prepared to stake yourself
on something being so.
—Arthur M. Ramsey

FAITH OR BELIEF: REASON, KNOWLEDGE, AND UNDERSTANDING

Faith doesn't wait until it understands; in that case it wouldn't be faith.

—Vance Havner

Reason is the triumph of the intellect, faith of the heart.

—James Schouler

Your faith is what you believe, not what you know.

—John Lancaster Spalding

Seek not to understand that thou mayest believe, but believe that thou mayest understand.

—Saint Augustine

Faith is a sounder guide than reason. Reason can go only so far, but faith has no limits.

—Blaise Pascal

It is faith, and not reason, which impels
men to action.... Intelligence is content
to point out the road, but never drives us
along it.

—Dr. Alexis Carrel

All the scholastic scaffolding falls, as a
ruined edifice, before a single word: faith.

—Napoleon Bonaparte

Some like to understand what they
believe in. Others like to believe in what
they understand.

—Stanislaus

It is the heart which experiences God,
and not the reason.

—Blaise Pascal

Faith is the continuation of reason.

—William Adams

Faith is a higher faculty than reason.

—Bailey

Faith is to believe what you do not yet
see; the reward for this faith is to see
what you believe.

—Saint Augustine

If life is a comedy to him who thinks,
and a tragedy to him who feels, it is a
victory to him who believes.

—Anon.

You're not free until you've been made
captive by supreme belief.

—Marianne Moore

It is by believing in roses that one brings
them to bloom.

—French proverb

Faith is believing when it is beyond the
power of reason to believe.

—Voltaire

Faith is reason grown courageous.

—Sherwood Eddy

It is as absurd to argue men, as to torture them, into believing.

—John Henry Cardinal Newman

Faith is believing what we cannot prove.

—Alfred, Lord Tennyson

Man makes holy what he believes, as he makes beautiful what he loves.

—Ernest Renan

If you wish to strive for peace of soul and pleasure, then believe.

—Heinrich Heine

The way to see by Faith is to shut the eye of Reason.

—Benjamin Franklin

If we were logical, the future would be bleak indeed. But we are more than logical. We are human beings, and we have faith, and we have hope.

—Jacques Cousteau

Faith is the result of the act of the will, following upon a conviction that to believe is a duty.

—John Henry Cardinal Newman

Reason's voice and God's, Nature's and Duty's, never are at odds.

—John Greenleaf Whittier

So often we have a kind of vague, wistful longing that the promises of Jesus should be true. The only way really to enter into them is to believe them with the clutching intensity of a drowning man.

—William Barclay

Faith is the art of holding on to things your reason has once accepted, in spite of your changing moods.

—C.S. Lewis

Reason is our soul's left hand, Faith her right. By this we reach divinity.

—John Donne

FAITH, DOUBT, AND FEAR

Doubt is a pain too lonely to know that
faith is his twin brother.
> —Kahlil Gibran

The only limit to our realization of
tomorrow will be our doubts of today.
Let us move forward with strong and
active faith.
> —Franklin Delano Roosevelt

Our faith triumphant o'er our fears.
> —Henry Wadsworth Longfellow

Fear imprisons, faith liberates; fear para-
lyzes, faith empowers; fear disheartens,
faith encourages; fear sickens, faith heals;
fear makes useless, faith makes service-
able.
> —Harry Emerson Fosdick

Faith which does not doubt is dead faith.
> —Miguel de Unamuno

O thou of little faith, why didst thou
doubt?
—Mt. 14:31

In the midst of your doubts, don't forget
how many of the important questions
God does answer.
—Verne Becker

It is impossible on reasonable grounds to
disbelieve miracles.
—Blaise Pascal

To believe with certainty we must begin
with doubting.
—Stanislaus I

Deep faith eliminates fear.
—Lech Walesa

Fear knocked at the door. Faith
answered. And lo, no one was there.
—Anon.

TRUSTING AND DARING

Faith is kind of like jumping out of an airplane at ten thousand feet. If God doesn't catch you, you splatter. But how do you know whether or not He is going to catch you unless you jump out?
—Ann Kiemel

Faith ... acts promptly and boldly on the occasion, on slender evidence.
—John Henry Cardinal Newman

The will of God will not take you where the grace of God cannot keep you.
—Anon.

Without risk, faith is an impossibility.
—Søren Kierkegaard

If it wasn't for faith, there would be no living in this world; we couldn't even eat hash with any safety.
—Josh Billings

The relation of faith between subject and object is unique in every case. Hundreds may believe, but each has to believe by himself.

—W.H. Auden

We cannot hand our faith to one another.... Even in the Middle Ages, when faith was theoretically uniform, it was always practically individual.

—John Jay Chapman

Let us move on, and step out boldly, though it be into the night, and we can scarcely see the way. A Higher Intelligence than the mortal sees the road before us.

—Charles B. Newcomb

Faith is an assent of the mind and a consent of the heart, consisting mainly of belief and trust.

—E.T. Hiscox

How to Develop Faith

Every human being is born without faith.
Faith comes only through the process of
making decisions to change before we
can be sure it's the right move.

—Dr. Robert H. Schuller

Seeds of discouragement will not grow in
the thankful heart.

—Anon.

Faith is not something to grasp, it is a
state to grow into.

—Mahatma Gandhi

To believe in God is to yearn for His
existence, and furthermore, it is to act as
if He did exist.

—Miguel de Unamuno

The principle part of faith is patience.

—George MacDonald

FAITH REQUIRES WORK AND EFFORT

Can a faith that does nothing be called sincere?

—Jean Racine

Faith without works is dead.

—Jas. 2:26

He does not believe who does not live according to his belief.

—Thomas Fuller

All effort is in the last analysis sustained by faith that it is worth making.

—Ordway Tweed

I have fought a good fight, I have finished my course, I have kept the faith.

—2 Tm. 4:7

To disbelieve is easy; to scoff is simple; to have faith is harder.

—Louis L'Amour

OTHER DEFINITIONS
OF FAITH AND BELIEF

Faith is a living and unshakable confidence, a belief in the grace of God so assured that a man would die a thousand deaths for its sake.

—Martin Luther

Faith is the subtle chain which binds us to the infinite.

—Elizabeth O. Smith

Faith is nothing but obedience and piety.

—Baruch Spinoza

Faith is a theological virtue that inclines the mind, under the influence of the will and grace, to yield firm assent to revealed truths, because of the authority of God.

—Adolphe Tanqueray

What's up is faith, what's down is heresy.

—Alfred, Lord Tennyson

Faith, to my mind, is a stiffening process, a sort of mental starch.

— E.M. Forster

Faith is love taking the form of aspiration.

— William Ellery Channing

Faith is hidden household capital.

— Johann von Goethe

Faith is that which is woven of conviction and set with the sharp mordant of experience.

— James Russell Lowell

Faith is the soul riding at anchor.

— Josh Billings

Faith is ... knowing with your heart.

— N. Richard Nash

Faith is the only known cure for fear.

— Lena K. Sadler

Faith is spiritualized imagination.
　　　　　　　—Henry Ward Beecher

Faith is the final triumph over incongruity, the final assertion of the meaningfulness of existence.
　　　　　　　—Reinhold Niebuhr

Faith is a certitude without proofs ... a sentiment, for it is a hope; it is an instinct, for it precedes all outward instruction.
　　　　　　　—Henry Frederic Amiel

Faith is an encounter in which God takes and keeps the initiative.
　　　　　　　—Eugene Joly

Faith is a practical attitude of the will.
　　　　　　　—John MacMurray

Faith is a total attitude of the self.
　　　　　　　—John Macquarrie

Faith is nothing else than trust in the divine mercy promised in Christ.
—Philipp Melanchthon

Faith is obedience, nothing else.
—Emil Brunner

Faith is a kind of betting, or speculation.
—Samuel Butler

Faith is the divine evidence whereby the spiritual man discerneth God, and the things of God.
—John Wesley

Faith is a passionate intuition.
—William Wordsworth

Faith is a bridge across the gulf of death.
—Edward Young

Faith is verification by the heart; confession by the tongue; action by the limbs.
—Anon.

Faith is the proper name of religious
experience.
      —John Baillie

Faith is an outward and visible sign of an
inward and spiritual grace.
    —*Book of Common Prayer*

Faith is the soul's adventure.
      —William Bridges

Faith is the response of our spirits to
beckonings of the eternal.
     —George A. Buttrick

Faith is a knowledge of the benevolence
of God toward us, and a certain persua-
sion of His veracity.
      —John Calvin

Faith is loyalty to some inspired teacher,
some spiritual hero.
     —Thomas Carlyle

Faith is God's work within us.
                    —Saint Thomas Aquinas

To me, faith means not worrying.
                    —John Dewey

Faith is building on what you know is here, so you can reach what you know is there.
                    —Cullen Hightower

Faith is a gift of God which man can neither give nor take away by promise of rewards, or menaces of torture.
                    —Thomas Hobbes

Faith is primarily a process of identification; the process by which the individual ceases to be himself and becomes part of something eternal.
                    —Eric Hoffer

Faith is the function of the heart.
                    —Mahatma Gandhi

Faith implies the disbelief of a lesser fact
in favor of a greater.
                    —Oliver Wendell Holmes

Faith is to believe in something not yet
proved and to underwrite it with our
lives: it is the only way we can leave the
future open.
                    —Lillian Smith

Faith begins as an experiment and ends
as an experience.
                    —William Ralph Inge

Faith is the little night-light that burns in
a sick-room; as long as it is there, the
obscurity is not complete, we turn
towards it and await the daylight.
                    —Abbé Henri Huvelin

Every tomorrow has two handles. We can
take hold of it by the handle of anxiety,
or by the handle of faith.
                    —Anon.

Faith is the summit of the Torah.
—Solomon Ibn Gabirol

Faith is not a storm cellar to which men
and women can flee for refuge from the
storms of life. It is, instead, an inner
force that gives them the strength to face
those storms and their consequences with
serenity of spirit.
—Sam J. Ervin, Jr.

Faith is an act of self-consecration, in
which the will, the intellect, and the
affections all have their place.
—William Ralph Inge

Faith is courage; it is creative, while
despair is always destructive.
—David S. Muzzey

Faith is an act of a finite being who is
grasped by, and turned to, the infinite.
—Paul Tillich

GENERAL QUOTATIONS ABOUT FAITH AND BELIEF

You can do very little with faith, but you can do nothing without it.

—Samuel Butler

A faith that sets bounds to itself, that will believe so much and no more, that will trust so far and no further, is none.

—Julius Charles Hare

The great act of faith is when a man decides that he is not God.

—Oliver Wendell Holmes

The opposite of having faith is having self-pity.

—Og Guinness

I am living on hope and faith ... a pretty good diet when the mind will receive them.

—Edwin Arlington Robinson

Be thou faithful unto death.

—Rev. 2:10

I would rather live in a world where my
life is surrounded by mystery than live in
a world so small that my mind could
comprehend it.

—Henry Emerson Fosdick

Faith is necessary to victory.

—William Hazlitt

The disease with which the human mind
now labors is want of faith.

—Ralph Waldo Emerson

Faith is a gift of God.

—Blaise Pascal

Faith assuages, guides, restores.

—Arthur Rimbaud

Loving is half of believing.

—Victor Hugo

Far graver is it to corrupt the faith that is the life of the soul than to counterfeit the money that sustains temporal life.

—Saint Thomas Aquinas

There is one inevitable criterion of judgment touching religious faith ... Can you reduce it to practice? If not, have none of it.

—Hosea Ballou

Pity the human being who is not able to connect faith within himself with the infinite.... He who has faith has ... an inward reservoir of courage, hope, confidence, calmness, and assuring trust that all will come out well—even though to the world it may appear to come out most badly.

—B.C. Forbes

No faith is our own that we have not arduously won.

—Havelock Ellis

To win true peace, a man needs to feel himself directed, pardoned and sustained by a supreme power, to feel himself in the right road, at the point where God would have him be—in order with God and the universe. This faith gives strength and calm.

—Henri Frederic Amiel

Strike from mankind the principle of faith, and men would have no more history than a flock of sheep.

—Edward Bulwer-Lytton

Faith is the force of life.

—Leo Tolstoy

Faith is the sturdiest, the most manly of the virtues. It lies behind our pluckiest ... strivings. It is the virtue of the storm, just as happiness is the virtue of the sunshine.

—Ruth Benedict

Faith may be relied upon to produce sustained action and, more rarely, sustained contemplation.

—Aldous Huxley

The person who has a firm trust in the Supreme Being is powerful in his power, wise by his wisdom, happy by his happiness.

—Joseph Addison

Faith is one of the forces by which men live; the total absence of it means collapse.

—William James

As your faith is strengthened you will find that there is no longer the need to have a sense of control, that things will flow as they will, and that you will flow with them, to your great delight and benefit.

—Emmanuel

Faith is putting all your eggs in God's basket, then counting your blessings before they hatch.

—Ramona C. Carroll

Something will turn up.

—Benjamin Disraeli

The historic glory of America lies in the fact that it is the one nation that was founded like a church. That is, it was founded on a faith that was not merely summed up after it had exited, but was defined before it existed.

—G.K. Chesterton

Through the dark and stormy night
Faith beholds a feeble light
Up the blackness streaking;
Knowing God's own time is best,
In a patient hope I rest
For the full day-breaking!

—John Greenleaf Whittier

The only faith that wears well and holds its color in all weather is that which is woven of conviction.

—James Russell Lowell

The primary cause of unhappiness in the world today is ... lack of faith.

—Carl Jung

You do build in darkness if you have faith. When the light returns you have made of yourself a fortress which is impregnable to certain kinds of trouble; you may even find yourself needed and sought by others as a beacon in their dark.

—Olga Rosmanith

It is by faith that poetry, as well as devotion, soars above this dull earth; that imagination breaks through its clouds, breathes a purer air, and lives in a softer light.

—Henry Giles

Religious faith, indeed, relates to that which is above us, but it must arise from that which is within us.

—Josiah Royce

Faith makes the discords of the present the harmonies of the future.

—Robert Collyer

A person consists of his faith. What-ever is his faith, even so is he.

—Hindu proverb

In Israel, in order to be a realist, you must believe in miracles.

—David Ben-Gurion

Living is a form of not being sure, not knowing what next, or how. The moment you know how, you begin to die a little. The artist never entirely knows. We guess. We may be wrong, but we take leap after leap in the dark.

—Agnes de Mille

For the believer, there is no question; for the non-believer, there is no answer.

—Anon.

Life without faith in something is too narrow a space in which to live.

—George Lancaster Spalding

PART THREE

PRAYER

WHY PRAY?

I pray on the principle that wine knocks
the cork out of a bottle. There is an
inward fermentation, and there must be
a vent.

—Henry Ward Beecher

They who have steeped their soul in
prayer can every anguish calmly bear.

—Richard M. Milnes

Unless I had the spirit of prayer, I could
do nothing.

—Charles G. Finney

Prayer is an end to isolation. It is living
our daily life with someone; with him
who alone can deliver us from solitude.

—Georges Lefevre

Prayer moves the hand that moves the
world.

—John Aikman Wallace

Prayer changes things.

—Anon.

Prayer does not change God, but it changes him who prays.

—Søren Kierkegaard

There is no hope but in prayer.

—Andrew Bonar

We can do nothing without prayer. All things can be done by importunate prayer. It surmounts or removes all obstacles, overcomes every resisting force and gains its ends in the face of invincible hindrances.

—E.M. Bounds

By prayer we couple the powers of heaven to our helplessness, the powers which can capture strongholds and make the impossible possible.

—O. Hallesby

Religion is no more possible without prayer than poetry without language or music without atmosphere.
—James Martineau

Faith, and hope, and patience and all the strong, beautiful, vital forces of piety are withered and dead in a prayerless life. The life of the individual believer, his personal salvation, and personal Christian graces have their being, bloom, and fruitage in prayer.
—E.M. Bounds

Every chain that spirits wear crumbles in the breadth of prayer.
—John Greenleaf Whittier

Oh, what a cause of thankfulness it is that we have a gracious God to go to on all occasions! Use and enjoy this privilege and you can never be miserable. Oh, what an unspeakable privilege is prayer!
—Lady Maxwell

God shapes the world by prayer. Prayers are deathless. They outlive the lives of those who uttered them.

—E.M. Bounds

To have a curable illness and to leave it untreated except for prayer is like sticking your hand in a fire and asking God to remove the flame.

—Sandra L. Douglas

Though we cannot by our prayers give God any information, yet we must by our prayers give him honor.

—Matthew Henry

In the war upon the powers of darkness, prayer is the primary and mightiest weapon, both in aggressive war upon them and their works; in the deliverance of men from their power; and against them as a hierarchy of powers opposed to Christ and His Church.

—Jessie Penn-Lewis

Men of God are always men of prayer.
—Henry T. Mahan

All who have walked with God have
viewed prayer as the main business of
their lives.
—Delma Jackson

Time spent on the knees in prayer will
do more to remedy heart strain and
nerve worry than anything else.
—George David Stewart

What is the life of a Christian but a life
of prayer!
—David Brown

Even if no command to pray had
existed, our very weakness would have
suggested it.
—Francois de Fenelon

He who ceases to pray ceases to prosper.
—Sir William Gurney Benham

By prayer, the ability is secured to feel the law of love, to speak according to the law of love, and to do everything in harmony with the law of love.

—E.M. Bounds

No heart thrives without much secret converse with God and nothing will make amends for the want of it.

—John Berridge

Prayer covers the whole of man's life. There is no thought, feeling, yearning, or desire, however low, trifling, or vulgar we may deem it, which, if it affects our real interest or happiness, we may not lay before God and be sure of sympathy. His nature is such that our often coming does not tire him. The whole burden of the whole life of every man may be rolled on to God and not weary him, though it has wearied the man.

—Henry Ward Beecher

The first purpose of prayer is to know
God.

—Charles L. Allen

No matter what may be the test,
God will take care of you;
Lean, weary one, upon His breast,
God will take care of you.

—C.D. Martin

Prayer is the great engine to overthrow
and rout my spiritual enemies, the great
means to procure the graces of which I
stand in hourly need.

—John Newton

Trouble and perplexity drive me to
prayer and prayer drives away perplexity
and trouble.

—Philipp Melanchthon

A man's state before God may always be
measured by his prayers.

—J.C. Ryle

No one is a firmer believer in the power of prayer than the devil; not that he practices it, but he suffers from it.

—Guy H. King

We, one and all of us, have an instinct to pray; and this fact constitutes an invitation from God to pray.

—Charles Sanders Peirce

The one concern of the devil is to keep Christians from praying. He fears nothing from prayerless studies, prayerless work, and prayerless religion. He laughs at our toil, mocks at our wisdom, but trembles when we pray.

—Samuel Chadwick

Teach us to pray that we may cause
The enemy to flee,
That we his evil power may bind,
His prisoners to free.

—Watchman Nee

The purpose of prayer is to reveal the presence of God equally present, all the time, in every condition.

—Oswald Chambers

Pray, always pray; when sickness wastes thy frame,
Prayer brings the healing power of Jesus' name.

—A.B. Simpson

Prayer honors God, acknowledges His being, exalts His power, adores His providence, secures His aid.

—E.M. Bounds

The value of consistent prayer is not that He will hear us, but that we will hear Him.

—William McGill

The whole meaning of prayer is that we may know God.

—Oswald Chambers

Prayer crowns God with the honor and glory due to His name, and God crowns prayer with assurance and comfort. The most praying souls are the most assured souls.

—Thomas B. Brooks

The goal of prayer is the ear of God, a goal that can only be reached by patient and continued and continuous waiting upon Him, pouring out our heart to Him and permitting Him to speak to us. Only by so doing can we expect to know Him, and as we come to know Him better we shall spend more time in His presence and find that presence a constant and ever-increasing delight.

—E.M. Bounds

He who has learned to pray has learned the greatest secret of a holy and a happy life.

—William Law

Non-praying is lawlessness, discord, anarchy.

—E.M. Bounds

The main lesson about prayer is just this: Do it! Do it! Do it! You want to be taught to pray? My answer is: pray.

—John Laidlaw

We look upon prayer as a means of getting things for ourselves; The Bible idea of prayer is that we may get to know God Himself.

—Oswald Chambers

Prayer is of transcendent importance. Prayer is the mightiest agent to advance God's work. Praying hearts and hands only can do God's work. Prayer succeeds when all else fails.

—E.M. Bounds

PRAYER IS PRACTICAL

The influence of prayer on the human mind and body ... can be measured in terms of increased physical buoyancy, greater intellectual vigor, moral stamina, and a deeper understanding of the realities underlying human relationships.

—Dr. Alexis Carrel

Prayer is not an old woman's idle amusement. Properly understood and applied, it is the most potent instrument of action.

—Mahatma Gandhi

Today any successful and competent businessman will employ the latest and best-tested methods in production, distribution, and administration, and many are discovering that one of the greatest of all efficiency methods is prayer power.

—Norman Vincent Peale

To have a curable illness and to leave it untreated except for prayer is like sticking your hand in a fire and asking God to remove the flame.

—Sandra L. Douglas

Prayer is the force as real as terrestrial gravity. As a physician, I have seen men, after all other therapy had failed, lifted out of disease and melancholy by the serene effort of prayer. Only in prayer do we achieve that complete and harmonious assembly of body, mind and spirit which gives the frail human reed its unshakable strength.

—Dr. Alexis Carrel

Tomorrow I plan to work, work, from early until late. In fact I have so much to do that I shall spend the first three hours in prayer.

—Martin Luther

PRAYER CHANGES US

One night alone in prayer might make us new men, changed from poverty of soul to spiritual wealth, from trembling to triumphing.

—Charles Haddon Spurgeon

Every time we pray our horizon is altered, our attitude to things is altered, not sometimes but every time, and the amazing thing is that we don't pray more.

—Oswald Chambers

It is not so true that "prayer changes things" as that prayer changes me and I change things. God has so constituted things that prayer on the basis of Redemption alters the way in which a man looks at things. Prayer is not a question of altering things externally, but of working wonders in a man's disposition.

—Oswald Chambers

How to Pray

When you cannot pray as you would,
pray as you can.
> —Edward M. Goulburn

If you can't pray as you want to, pray as
you can. God knows what you mean.
> —Vance Havner

Praying is learned by praying.
> —L.A.T. van Dooren

The only way to pray is to pray, and the
way to pray well is to pray much.
> —Anon.

The less I pray, the harder it gets; the
more I pray, the better it goes.
> —Martin Luther

Pray till you pray.
> —D.M. McIntyre

All the prayers in the Scripture you will find to be reasoning with God, not a multitude of words heaped together.
—Stephen Charnock

The great thing in prayer is to feel that we are putting our supplications into the bosom of omnipotent love.
—Andrew Murray

You need not cry very loud; he is nearer to us than we think.
—Brother Lawrence

Scream at God if that's the only thing that will get results.
—Brendan Francis

It has been well said that almost the only scoffers at prayer are those who never tried it enough.
—*Twelve Steps and Twelve Traditions*

Prayer is a trade to be learned. We must
be apprentices and serve our time at it.
Painstaking care, much thought, practice
and labour are required to be a skillful
tradesman in praying. Practice in this, as
well as in all other trades, makes perfect.
　　　　　　　　　　　—E.M. Bounds

If we are willing to spend hours on end
to learn to play the piano, operate a com-
puter, or fly an airplane, it is sheer non-
sense for us to imagine that we can learn
the high art of getting guidance through
communion with the Lord without being
willing to set aside time for it.
　　　　　　　　　　　　—Paul Rees

He that will learn to pray, let him to sea.
　　　　　　　　　　—George Herbert

Rejoice always, pray constantly, and in all
circumstances give thanks.
　　　　　　　　　—The Desert Fathers

Incense is prayer
That drives no bargain.
Child, learn from incense
How best to pray.

—Alfred Barrett

Natural ability and educational advantages do not figure as factors in this matter of prayer; but a capacity for faith, the
power of a thorough consecration, the
ability of self-littleness, an absolute losing
of one's self in God's glory and an ever
present and insatiable yearning and seeking after all the fullness of God.

—E.M. Bounds

Do I want to pray or only to think
about my human problems? Do I want
to pray or simply kneel there contemplating my sorrow? Do I want to direct
my prayer toward God or let it direct
itself towards me?

—Hubert Van Zeller

O thou, by whom we come to God,
The Life, the Truth, the Way,
The path of prayer Thyself hast trod—
Lord teach us how to pray.
                          —James Montgomery

The right way to pray, then, is any way
that allows us to communicate with God.
                          —Colleen Townsend Evans

Confess your faults one to another, and
pray one for another, that ye may be
healed. The effectual, fervent prayer of a
righteous man availeth much.
                          —Jas. 5:16

We have to pray with our eyes on God,
not on the difficulties.
                          —Oswald Chambers

Grant us grace, Almighty Father, so to
pray as to deserve to be heard.
                          —Jane Austen

When we go to our meeting with God, we should go like a patient to his doctor, first to be thoroughly examined and afterwards to be treated for our ailment. Then something will happen when you pray.

—O. Hallesby

He prayeth well, who loveth well
Both man and bird and beast.
He prayeth best, who loveth best
All things both great and small;
For the dear God who loveth us,
He made and loveth all.

—Samuel Taylor Coleridge

God tells us to burden him with whatever burdens us.

—Anon.

Dealing in generalities is the death of prayer.

—J.H. Evans

To pray is nothing more involved than to open the door, giving Jesus access to our needs and permitting Him to exercise His own power in dealing with them.

—O. Hallesby

If our petitions are in accordance with His will, and if we seek His glory in the asking, the answers will come in ways that will astonish us and fill our hearts with songs of thanksgiving.

—J.K. Maclean

He prays best who does not know that he is praying.

—Saint Anthony of Padua

Pray if thou canst with hope, but ever pray, though hope be weak or sick with long delay; pray in the darkness if there be no light; and if for any wish thou dare not pray, then pray to God to cast that wish away.

—Anon.

DAILY PRAYER

A day without prayer is a boast against
God.

—Owen Carr

In the morning, prayer is the key that
opens to us the treasures of God's mercies
and blessings; in the evening, it is the key
that shuts us up under His protection
and safeguard.

—Anon.

O God, if in the day of battle I forget
Thee, do not Thou forget me.

—Anon.

Seven days without prayer makes one
weak.

—Allen E. Bartlett

Prayer should be the key of the day and
the lock of the night.

—Thomas Fuller

Prayer is a kind of calling home every day. And there can come to you a serenity, a feeling of at-homeness in God's universe, a peace that the world can neither give nor disturb, a fresh courage, a new insight, a holy boldness that you'll never get any other way.

—Earl G. Hunt, Jr.

Let it be your business every day, in the secrecy of the inner chamber, to meet the holy God. You will be repaid for the trouble it may cost you. The reward will be sure and rich.

—Andrew Murray

Prayer should be the means by which I, at all times, receive all that I need, and, for this reason, be my daily refuge, my daily consolation, my daily joy, my source of rich and inexhaustible joy in life.

—Saint John Chrysostom

We read of preaching the Word out of season, but we do not read of praying out of season, for that is never out of season.

—Matthew Henry

I care not what black spiritual crisis we may come through or what delightful spiritual Canaan we may enter, no blessing of the Christian life becomes continually possessed unless we are men and women of regular, daily, unhurried, secret lingerings in prayer.

—J. Sidlow Baxter

Lord, you know how busy I must be this day. If I forget you, do not you forget me.

—Jacob Astley

Evening, and morning, and at noon, will I pray.

—Ps. 55:17

CONTINUAL PRAYER

As impossible as it is for us to take a
breath in the morning large enough to
last us until noon, so impossible is it to
pray in the morning in such a way as to
last us until noon. Let your prayers
ascend to Him constantly, audibly or
silently, as circumstances throughout the
day permit.

—O. Hallesby

Abiding fully means praying much.

—Andrew Murray

To God your every Want
In instant Prayer display,
Pray always; Pray, and never faint;
Pray, without ceasing, Pray.

—Charles Wesely

Constant prayer quickly straightens out
our thoughts.

—The Desert Fathers

Teach us to pray often, that we may pray oftener.

—Jeremy Taylor

Time spent in prayer is never wasted.

—Francois de Fenelon

Pray, always pray; beneath sins heaviest
   load,
Prayer claims the blood from Jesus' side
   that flowed.
Pray, always pray; though weary, faint,
   and lone,
Prayer nestles by the Father's sheltering
   throne.

—A.B. Simpson

When the knees are not often bent, the feet soon slide.

—Anon.

The more praying there is in the world, the better the world will be; the mightier the forces against evil everywhere.

—E.M. Bounds

WE MUST MAKE TIME TO PRAY

I have to hurry all day to get time to
pray.

—Martin Luther

When it becomes clear to us that prayer
is a part of our daily program of work, it
will also become clear to us that we must
arrange our daily program in such a way
that there is time also for this work, just
as we set aside time for other necessary
things, such as eating and dressing.

—O. Hallesby

Sometimes we think we are too busy to
pray. That is a great mistake, for praying
is a saving of time.

—Charles Haddon Spurgeon

Prayer time must be kept up as duly as
meal-time.

—Matthew Henry

The minds of people are so cluttered up with every-day living these days that they don't, or won't, take time out for a little prayer—for mental cleansing, just as they take a bath for physical, outer cleansing. Both are necessary.

—Jo Ann Carlson

The Christian will find his parentheses for prayer even in the busiest hours of life.

—Richard Cecil

No time is so well spent in every day as that which we spend upon our knees.

—J.C. Ryle

Other duties become pressing and absorbing and crowd our prayer. "Choked to death" would be the coroner's verdict in many cases of dead praying if an inquest could be secured on this dire, spiritual calamity.

—E.M. Bounds

It is impossible to conduct your life as a
disciple without definite times of secret
prayer.

—Oswald Chambers

If you are swept off your feet, it's time to
get on your knees.

—Fred Beck

Jesus, please teach me to appreciate what
I have before time forces me to appreciate what I had.

—Susan L. Lenzkes

Begin to realize more and more that
prayer is the most important thing you
do. You can use your time to no better
advantage than to pray whenever you
have an opportunity to do so, either
alone or with others; while at work,
while at rest, or while walking down the
street. Anywhere!

—O. Hallesby

MORNING PRAYER

Temptations which accompany the working day will be conquered on the basis of the morning breakthrough to God. Decisions, demanded by work, become easier and simpler where they are made not in the fear of men, but only in the sight of God. He wants to give us today the power which we need for our work.

—Dietrich Bonhoeffer

While others still slept, He went away to pray and to renew His strength in communion with His Father. He had need of this, otherwise He would not have been ready for the new day. The holy work of delivering souls demands constant renewal through fellowship with God.

—Andrew Murray

In the morning will I direct my prayer unto thee.

—Ps. 5:3

If you have ever prayed in the dawn you will ask yourself why you were so foolish as not to do it always: it is difficult to get into communion with God in the midst of the hurly-burly of the day.

—Oswald Chambers

And in the morning, rising up a great while before day, he went out, and departed into a solitary place, and there prayed.

—Mk. 1:35

It is by no haphazard chance that in every age men have risen early to pray. The first thing that marks decline in spiritual life is our relationship to the early morning.

—Oswald Chambers

Lord, if any have to die this day, let it be me, for I am ready.

—Billy Bray

The entire day receives order and discipline when it acquires unity. This unity must be sought and found in morning prayer. The morning prayer determines the day.

—Dietrich Bonhoeffer

Cause me to hear thy loving kindness in the morning.

—Psalms

Thank God every morning when you get up that you have something to do which must be done, whether you like it or not.

—Charles Kingsley

I feel it is far better to begin with God, to see His face first, to get my soul near Him before it is near another. In general it is best to have at least one hour alone with God before engaging in anything else.

—E.M. Bounds

EVENING PRAYER

The man who says his prayers in the
evening is a captain posting his sentries.
After that, he can sleep.

> —Charles Baudelaire

Keep us, Lord, so awake in the duties of
our calling that we may sleep in thy
peace and wake in thy glory.

> —John Donne

I did this night promise my wife never to
go to bed without calling upon God,
upon my knees, in prayer.

> —Samuel Pepys

When at night you cannot sleep, talk to
the Shepherd and stop counting sheep.

> —Anon.

Praying When We Bottom Out

Prayer may not change things for you,
but it for sure changes you for things.
—Samuel M. Shoemaker

"Oh, God, if I were sure I were to die
tonight I would repent at once." It is the
commonest prayer in all languages.
—Sir James M. Barrie

When I am weak, then am I strong.
—2 Cor. 12:10

Prayer begins where human capacity
ends.
—Marian Anderson

To pray is to open the door unto Jesus
and admit Him into your distress. Your
helplessness is the very thing which
opens wide the door unto Him and gives
Him access to all your needs.
—O. Hallesby

I have been driven many times to my
knees by the overwhelming conviction
that I had nowhere else to go. My own
wisdom and that of all about me seemed
insufficient for the day.

—Abraham Lincoln

Ordinarily when a man in difficulty
turns to prayer, he has already tried every
other means of escape.

—Austin O'Malley

Now I am past all comforts here, but
prayer.

—William Shakespeare

My helpless friend, your helplessness is
the most powerful plea which rises up to
the tender father-heart of God. You think
that everything is closed to you because
you cannot pray. My friend, your helplessness is the very essence of prayer.

—O. Hallesby

When a man is at his wits' end it is not a cowardly thing to pray, it is the only way he can get in touch with Reality.

—Oswald Chambers

Listen, my friend! Your helplessness is your best prayer. It calls from your heart to the heart of God with greater effect than all your uttered pleas. He hears it from the very moment that you are seized with helplessness, and He becomes actively engaged at once in hearing and answering the prayer of your helplessness.

—O. Hallesby

When my soul fainted within me ... my prayer came in unto thee.

—Jon. 2:7

Trouble and prayer are closely related.... Trouble often drives men to God in prayer, while prayer is but the voice of men in trouble.

—E.M. Bounds

When we pray for the Spirit's help ... we will simply fall down at the Lord's feet in our weakness. There we will find the victory and power that comes from His love.

—Andrew Murray

God listens to our weeping when the occasion itself is beyond our knowledge, but still within His love and power.

—Daniel A. Poling

Trouble and perplexity drive me to prayer and prayer drives away perplexity and trouble.

—Philipp Melanchthon

Helplessness is unquestionably the first and the surest indication of a praying heart.... Prayer and helplessness are inseparable. Only he who is helpless can truly pray.

—O. Hallesby

Being in an agony, he prayed more
earnestly.

—Lk. 22:44

He will regard the prayer of the destitute.

—Ps. 102:17

Just pray for a tough hide and a tender
heart.

—Ruth Graham

Don't pray to escape trouble. Don't pray
to be comfortable in your emotions. Pray
to do the will of God in every situation.
Nothing else is worth praying for.

—Samuel M. Shoemaker

The more helpless you are, the better you
are fitted to pray, and the more answers
to prayer you will experience.

—O. Hallesby

My strength is made perfect in weakness.

—2 Cor. 12:9

But We Can't Pray Just
When We're in Trouble

All those football coaches who hold
dressing-room prayers before a game
should be forced to attend church once
a week.

—Duffy Daugherty

He who cannot pray when the sun is
shining will not know how to pray when
the clouds come.

—Anon.

You pray in your distress and in your
need; would that you might also pray in
the fullness of your joy and in your days
of abundance.

—Kahlil Gibran

Many people pray as if God were a big
aspirin pill; they come only when they
hurt.

—B. Graham Dienert

An agnostic found himself in trouble, and a friend suggested he pray. "How can I pray when I do not know whether or not there is a God?" he asked. "If you are lost in the forest," his friend replied, "you do not wait until you find someone before shouting for help."

—Dan Plies

Fear of trouble, present and future, often blinds us to the numerous small blessings we enjoy, silencing our prayers of praise and thanksgiving.

—Anon.

Don't pray when it rains if you don't pray when the sun shines.

—Satchel Paige

Prayer is not merely an occasional impulse to which we respond when we are in trouble: prayer is a life attitude.

—Walter A. Mueller

A Special Place for Prayer

Do not have as your motive the desire to
be known as a praying man. Get an inner
chamber in which to pray where no one
knows you are praying, shut the door,
and talk to God in secret.

—Oswald Chambers

But thou, when thou prayest, enter into
thy room, and when thou hast shut thy
door, pray to thy Father who is in secret;
and thy Father who seeth in secret, shall
reward thee openly.

—Mt. 6:6

Of all things, guard against neglecting
God in the secret place of prayer.

—William Wilberforce

Private place and plenty of time are the
life of prayer.

—E.M. Bounds

Nowhere can we get to know the holiness of God, and come under His influence and power, except in the inner chamber. It has been well said: "No man can expect to make progress in holiness who is not often and long alone with God."

—Andrew Murray

When you enter your secret chamber, take plenty of time before you begin to speak. Let quietude wield its influence upon you. Let the fact that you are alone assert itself. Give your soul time to get released from the many outward things. Give God time to play the prelude to prayer for the benefit of your distracted soul.

—O. Hallesby

There is no need to get to a place of prayer; pray wherever you are.

—Oswald Chambers

OUR PRAYERS SHOULD BE SINCERE, AND JIBE WITH HOW WE LIVE DAY TO DAY

Prayer, to the patriarchs and prophets, was more than the recital of well-known and well-worn phrases—it was the outpouring of the heart.

—Herbert Lockyer

The Lord's Prayer may be committed to memory quickly, but it is slowly learnt by heart.

—Frederick Denison Maurice

Sincerity is the prime requisite in every approach to the God who ... hates all hypocrisy, falsehood, and deceit.

—Geoffrey B. Wilson

Many pray with their lips for that for which their hearts have no desire.

—Jonathan Edwards

Without the incense of heartfelt prayer,
even the greatest of cathedrals is dead.

—Anon.

Prayers not felt by us are seldom heard
by God.

—Philip Henry

God hears no more than the heart
speaks; and if the heart be dumb, God
will certainly be dumb.

—Thomas B. Brooks

Do not pray by heart, but with the heart.

—Anon.

Heaven is never deaf but when man's
heart is dumb.

—Francis Quarles

Deep down in me I knowed it was a lie,
and He knowed it. You can't pray a lie—I
found that out.

—Mark Twain

God may turn his ears from prattling prayers, or preaching prayers, but never from penitent, believing prayers.

—William S. Plumer

Two went to pray? Better to say one went to brag, the other to pray.

—Richard Crashaw

I pray like a robber asking alms at the door of a farmhouse to which he is ready to set fire.

—Leon Bloy

We must lay before him what is in us, not what ought to be in us.

—C.S. Lewis

God's ear lies close to the believer's lip.

—Anon.

Our prayers must mean something to us if they are to mean anything to God.

—Maltbie D. Babcock

Our prayers must spring from the indigenous soil of our own personal confrontation with the Spirit of God in our lives.

—Malcolm Boyd

Prayer is a serious thing. We may be taken at our words.

—Dwight L. Moody

Prayer at its best is the expression of the total life, for all things else being equal, our prayers are only as powerful as our lives.

—A.W. Tozer

God eagerly awaits the chance to bless the person whose heart is turned toward Him.

—Anon.

In prayer the lips ne'er act the winning part, without the sweet concurrence of the heart.

—Robert Herrick

And help us, this and every day, to live more nearly as we pray.

—John Keble

Men would pray better if they lived better. They would get more from God if they lived more obedient and well-pleasing to God.

—E.M. Bounds

My words fly up, my thoughts remain
   below;
Words without thoughts never to heaven
   go.

—William Shakespeare

Prayer is the soul's sincere desire.

—James Montgomery

The cry of a young raven is nothing but the natural cry of a creature, but your cry, if it be sincere, is the result of a work of grace in your heart.

—Charles Haddon Spurgeon

It is not well for a man to pray cream and live skim milk.

—Henry Ward Beecher

She heard the snuffle of hypocrisy in her prayer. She had to cease to pray.

—George Meredith

Every time you pray, if your prayer is sincere, there will be new feeling and new meaning in it which will give you fresh courage, and you will understand that prayer is an education.

—Fyodor Dostoyevsky

He who prays as he ought, will endeavor to live as he prays.

—John Owen

We pray pious blether, our will is not in it, and then we say God does not answer; we never asked Him for anything. Asking means that our wills are in what we ask.

—Oswald Chambers

Praying which does not result in pure conduct is a delusion. We have missed the whole office and virtue of praying if it does not rectify conduct. It is in the very nature of things that we must quit praying, or quit bad conduct.

—E.M. Bounds

When you pray, rather let your heart be without words than your words without heart.

—John Bunyan

He offered a prayer so deeply devout that he seemed kneeling and praying at the bottom of the sea.

—Herman Melville

None can pray well but he that lives well.

—Thomas Fuller

Straight praying is never born of crooked conduct.

—E.M. Bounds

A wicked man in prayer may lift up his hands, but he cannot lift up his face.
—Thomas Watson

We cannot talk to God strongly when we have not lived for God strongly. The closet cannot be made holy to God when the life has not been holy to God.
—E.M. Bounds

It is good for us to keep some account of our prayers, that we may not unsay them in our practice.
—Matthew Henry

Search me, O God, and know my heart: try me, and know my thoughts: and see if there be any wicked way in me.
—Ps. 139:23–24

When our will wholeheartedly enters into the prayer of Christ, then we pray correctly.
—Dietrich Bonhoeffer

Be not hot in prayer and cold in praise.
                              —Anon.

Though smooth be the heartless prayer,
no ear in heaven will mind it;
And the finest phrase falls dead, if there
is no feeling behind it.
                    —Ella Wheeler Wilcox

If we would have God in the closet, God
must have us out of the closet. There is
no way of praying to God, but by living
to God.
                              —E.M. Bounds

Prayer is the soul's sincere desire,
Uttered, or unexpressed;
The motion of a hidden fire
That trembles in the breast.
                    —James Montgomery

Our Prayers Needn't Be Eloquent

We cannot all argue, but we can all pray; we cannot all be leaders, but we can all be pleaders; we cannot all be mighty in rhetoric, but we can all be prevalent in prayer.

—Charles Haddon Spurgeon

God can pick sense out of a confused prayer.

—Richard Sibbes

God prefers bad verses recited with a pure heart to the finest verses chanted by the wicked.

—Voltaire

We ought to act with God in the greatest simplicity, speak to Him frankly and plainly, and implore His assistance in our affairs.

—Brother Lawrence

Prayer is not eloquence, but earnestness; not the definition of helplessness, but the feeling of it; not figures of speech, but earnestness of soul.

—Hannah More

If we rely on the Holy Spirit, we shall find that our prayers become more and more inarticulate; and when they are inarticulate, reverence grows deeper and deeper.

—Oswald Chambers

In prayer it is better to have a heart without words than words without a heart.

—John Bunyan

Prayer is something deeper than words. It is present in the soul before it has been formulated in words. And it abides in the soul after the last words of prayer have passed over our lips.

—O. Hallesby

Productive prayer requires earnestness,
not eloquence.

—Anon.

The best prayers have often more groans
than words.

—John Bunyan

They tell about a fifteen-year-old boy in
an orphans' home who had an incurable
stutter. One Sunday the minister was
detained and the boy volunteered to say
the prayer in his stead. He did it per-
fectly, too, without a single stutter. Later
he explained, "I don't stutter when I talk
to God. He loves me."

—Bennett Cerf

Prayer is not artful monologue
Of voice uplifted from the son;
It is Love's tender dialogue
Between the soul and God.

—John Richard Moreland

THE BEST PRAYERS
ARE OFTEN BRIEF

Short prayers pierceth Heaven.
—The Cloud of Unknowing

The fewer the words, the better the prayer.
—Martin Luther

There come times when I have nothing more to tell God. If I were to continue to pray in words, I would have to repeat what I have already said. At such times it is wonderful to say to God, "May I be in Thy presence, Lord? I have nothing more to say to Thee, but I do love to be in Thy presence."
—O. Hallesby

God is in heaven, and thou upon earth: therefore let thy words be few.
—Eccl. 5:2

A little lifting of the heart suffices; a little remembrance of God, one act of inward worship are prayers which, however short, are nevertheless acceptable to God.

—Brother Lawrence

Productive prayer requires earnestness, not eloquence.

—Anon.

Many words do not a good prayer make; what counts is the heartfelt desire to commune with God, and the faith to back it up.

—Anon.

Prayer should be short, without giving God Almighty reasons why He should grant this or that; He knows best what is good for us.

—John Selden

ASKING FOR THINGS
THROUGH PRAYER

You are coming to a King,
Large petitions with you bring
For his grace and power are such
None can ever ask too much.
—John Newton

Most Christians expect little from God,
ask little, and therefore receive little and
are content with little.
—A.W. Pink

Ye have not, because ye ask not.
—Js. 4:2

God never denied that soul anything that
went as far as heaven to ask it.
—John Trapp

Whether we like it or not, asking is the
rule of the Kingdom.
—Charles Haddon Spurgeon

The simple heart that freely asks in love, obtains.

—John Greenleaf Whittier

Ask in faith.

—Jas. 1:6

The clue is not to ask in a miserly way— the key is to ask in a grand manner.

—Ann Wigmore

Let your requests be made known unto God.

—Phil. 4:6

To avail yourself of His certain wisdom, ask of Him whatever questions you have. But do not entreat Him, for that will never be necessary.

—Hugh Prather

Ye ask, and receive not, because ye ask amiss.

—Js. 4:3

Ask, and it shall be given you; seek, and ye shall find; knock, and it shall be opened unto you.

—Mt. 7:7

Pray for whatsoever you will. In the name of Jesus you have permission, not only to stand in the presence of God, but also to pray for everything you need.

—O. Hallesby

And whatever ye shall ask in my name, that will I do.

—1 Jn. 14:13

O Lord, attend unto my cry.

—Psalms

We pray pious blether, our will is not in it, and then we say God does not answer; we never asked Him for anything. Asking means that our wills are in what we ask.

—Oswald Chambers

Ask the gods nothing excessive.

—Aeschylus

When praying for healing, ask great
things of God and expect great things
from God. But let us seek for that healing that really matters, the healing of the
heart, enabling us to trust God simply,
face God honestly, and live triumphantly.

—Arlo F. Newell

Most people do not pray; they only beg.

—Bernard Shaw

Prayer is not asking. It is a longing of the
soul.

—Mahatma Gandhi

Prayer in the sense of petition, asking for
things, is a small part of it; confession
and penitence are its threshold, adoration
its sanctuary, the presence and vision and
enjoyment of God its bread and wine.

—C.S. Lewis

SELFISHNESS AND PRAYER

If your prayer is selfish, the answer will be something that will rebuke your self-ishness. You may not recognize it as having come at all, but it is sure to be there.

—William Temple

Selfishness is never so exquisitely selfish as when it is on its knees.... Self turns what would otherwise be a pure and powerful prayer into a weak and ineffective one.

—A.W. Tozer

I seldom made an errand to God for another but I got something for myself.

—Samuel Rutherford

When we make self the end of prayer, it is not worship but self-seeking.

—Thomas Manton

We Should Pray for Others

Pray for one another.

—Jas. 5:16

Intercessory prayer for one who is sinning prevails. God says so! The will of the man prayed for does not come into question at all, he is connected with God by prayer, and prayer on the basis of the Redemp-tion sets the connection working and God gives life.

—Oswald Chambers

See to it, night and day, that you pray for your children. Then you will leave them a great legacy of answers to prayer, which will follow them all the days of their life. Then you may calmly and with a good conscience depart from them, even though you may not leave them a great deal of material wealth.

—O. Hallesby

If we could all hear one another's prayers,
God might be relieved of some of his
burden.

—Ashleigh Brilliant

God bless all those that I love; God bless
all those that love me; God bless all those
that love those that I love and all those
that love those that love me.

—A New England Sampler

If we do not love one another, we certainly shall not have much power with
God in prayer.

—Dwight L. Moody

He who prays for his neighbors will be
heard for himself.

—Talmud

No one who has had a unique experience
with prayer has a right to withhold it
from others.

—Soong Mel-Ling

GRATITUDE

Thou who has given so much to me, give
one thing more: a grateful heart.
—George Herbert

If the only prayer you say in your whole
life is "Thank you," that would suffice.
—Meister Eckhart

For food, for raiment, for life and opportunity, for sun and rain, for water and
the portage trails, we give you thanks, O
Lord.
—A Prayer from the North Woods

God deserves far more praise than any of
us could ever give Him.
—Anon.

Our Father, let the spirit of gratitude so
prevail in our hearts that we may mani-
fest thy Spirit in our lives.
—W.B. Slack

Our thanks to God should always precede our requests.

—Anon.

To stand on one leg and prove God's existence is a very different thing from going down on one's knees and thanking him.

—Søren Kierkegaard

It is not only blessed to give thanks; it is also of vital importance to our prayer life in general. If we have noted the Lord's answers to our prayers and thanked Him for what we have received of Him, then it becomes easier for us, and we get more courage, to pray for more.

—O. Hallesby

A sensible thanksgiving for mercies received is a mighty prayer in the Spirit of God. It prevails with Him unspeakably.

—John Bunyan

Pray without ceasing. In everything give thanks.

—1 Th. 5:17

Let us thank God heartily as often as we pray that we have His Spirit in us to teach us to pray. Thanksgiving will draw our hearts out to God and keep us engaged with Him; it will take our attention from ourselves and give the Spirit room in our hearts.

—Andrew Murray

God receives little thanks, even for his greatest gifts.

—Anon.

Do not want things to turn out as they seem best to you, but as God pleases. Then you will be free from confusion, and thankful in prayer.

—The Desert Fathers

Let us come before his presence with thanksgiving.

—Ps. 95:2

ENTHUSIASTIC PRAYING

Don't be timid when you pray; rather, batter the very gates of heaven with storms of prayer.

—Anon.

Look, as a painted man is no man, and as painted fire is no fire, so a cold prayer is no prayer.

—Thomas B. Brooks

There must be fired affections before our prayers will go up.

—William Jenkyn

Cold prayers shall never have any warm answers.

—Thomas B. Brooks

We must wrestle earnestly in prayer, like men contending with a deadly enemy for life.

—J.C. Ryle

How those holy men of old could storm the battlements above! When there was no way to look but up, they lifted up their eyes to God who made the hills, with unshakable confidence.

—Herbert Lockyer

We may as well not pray at all as offer our prayers in a lifeless manner.

—William S. Plumer

There is neither encouragement nor room in Bible religion for feeble desires, listless efforts, lazy attitudes; all must be strenuous, urgent, ardent. Flamed desires, impassioned, unwearied insistence delight heaven. God would have His children incorrigibly in earnest and persistently bold in their efforts. Heaven is too busy to listen to half-hearted prayers or to respond to pop-calls. Our whole being must be in our praying.

—E.M. Bounds

The effectual, fervent prayer of a right-eous man availeth much.

—Jas. 5:16

From silly devotions and from sour-faced saints, good Lord, deliver us.

—Saint Teresa of Avila

Let me burn out for God ... prayer is the great thing. Oh, that I may be a man of prayer!

—Henry Martyn

Bear up the hands that hang down, by faith and prayer; support the tottering knees. Storm the throne of grace and persevere therein, and mercy will come down.

—John Wesley

Do not work so hard for Christ that you have no strength to pray, for prayer requires strength.

—J. Hudson Taylor

THINGS TO PRAY FOR

We must move from asking God to take
care of the things that are breaking our
hearts, to praying about the things that
are breaking His heart.

—Margaret Gibb

Our prayers should be for blessings in
general, for God knows best what is good
for us.

—Socrates

Not what we wish, but what we need,
Oh! let your grace supply,
The good unasked, in mercy grant;
The ill, though asked, deny.

—James Merrik

We cannot ask in behalf of Christ what
Christ would not ask Himself if He were
praying.

—A.B. Simpson

Thou who has given so much to me, give one thing more: a grateful heart.

—George Herbert

God's promises are to be our pleas in prayer.

—Matthew Henry

O Lord, help me not to despise or oppose what I do not understand.

—William Penn

If we are to pray aright, perhaps it is quite necessary that we pray contrary to our own heart. Not what we want to pray is important, but what God wants us to pray. The richness of the Word of God ought to determine our prayer, not the poverty of our heart.

—Dietrich Bonhoeffer

For we know not what we should pray for.

—Rom. 8:26

We are going home to many who cannot read. So, Lord, make us to be Bibles so that those who cannot read the Book can read it in us.

—Anonymous Chinese woman

The whole meaning of prayer is that we may know God.

—Oswald Chambers

We must pray for more prayer, for it is the world's mightiest healing force.

—Frank C. Laubach

O Lord, let me not live to be useless!

—Bishop John de Stratford

We should pray for a sane mind in a sound body.

—Juvenal

We do pray for mercy, and that same prayer doth teach us all to render the deeds of mercy.

—William Shakespeare

Lord, take my lips and speak through
them; take my mind and think through
it; take my heart and set it on fire.
—W.H. Aitken

Grant that we may not so much seek to
be understood as to understand.
—Saint Francis of Assisi

God give me work, till my life shall end
And life, till my work is done.
—Winifred Holtby's epitaph

The first petition that we are to make to
Almighty God is for a good conscience,
the next for health of mind, and then of
body.
—Lucius Annaeius Seneca

Give us Lord, a bit o'sun,
A bit o'work, and a bit o'fun;
Give us all, in the struggle and sputter
Our daily bread and a bit o'butter.
—On an old inn, Lancaster, England

Watch your motive before God; have no other motive in prayer than to know Him.

—Oswald Chambers

Pray a little each day in a childlike way for the Spirit of prayer. If you feel that you know, as yet, very little concerning the deep things of prayer and what prayer really is, then pray for the Spirit of prayer. There is nothing He would rather do than unveil to you the grace of prayer.

—O. Hallesby

God does not exist to answer our prayers, but by our prayers we come to discern the mind of God.

—Oswald Chambers

I sit beside my lonely fire and pray for wisdom yet: for calmness to remember or courage to forget.

—Charles Hamilton Aide

The purpose of prayer is not to inform God of our needs, but to invite Him to rule our lives.

—Clarence Bauman

Grant me the courage not to give up, even though I think it is hopeless.

—Admiral Chester W. Nimitz

Do not forget that prayer is ordained for the purpose of glorifying the name of God. Therefore, whether you pray for big things or for little things, say to God, "If it will glorify Thy name, then grant my prayer and help me."

—O. Hallesby

Prayer for worldly goods is worse than fruitless, but prayer for strength of soul is that passion of the soul which catches the gift it seeks.

—George Meredith

WE SHOULD PRAY
TO DO GOD'S WILL

O Lord, forgive what I have been, sanctify what I am, and order what I shall be.
—Anon.

The possibilities of prayer are found in its allying itself with the purposes of God, for God's purposes and man's praying are the combination of all potent and omnipotent forces.
—E.M. Bounds

How many of us will ever sit ... bow our heads, and pray "Lord, show me where I'm wrong"?
—Anon.

I would have no desire other than to accomplish thy will. Teach me to pray; pray thyself in me.
—Francois de Fenelon

True prayer brings a person's will into accordance with God's will, not the other way around.

—Anon.

I used to pray that God would do this or that; now I pray that God will make His will known to me.

—Madame Chiang Kai-Shek

O Lord, you know what is best for me. Let this or that be done, as you please. Give what you will, how much you will, and when you will.

—Thomas a'Kempis

Spread out your petition before God, and then say, "Thy will, not mine, be done." The sweetest lesson I have learned in God's school is to let the Lord choose for me.

—Dwight L. Moody

WE SHOULDN'T PRAY FOR THE END OF PROBLEMS, BUT FOR THE ABILITY TO HANDLE THEM

Do not pray for easy lives, pray to be stronger men. Do not pray for tasks equal to your powers, pray for powers equal to your tasks.

—Phillips Brooks

Pray not for lighter burdens, but for stronger backs.

—Theodore Roosevelt

The wise man in the storm prays God not for safety from danger, but for deliverance from fear.

—Ralph Waldo Emerson

It is quite useless knocking at the door of heaven for earthly comfort. It's not the sort of comfort they supply there.

—C.S. Lewis

TURNING THINGS OVER
THROUGH PRAYER

I know not by what methods rare,
But this I know: God answers prayer.
I know not if the blessing sought
Will come in just the guise I thought.
I leave my prayer to Him alone
Whose will is wiser than my own.
                              —Eliza M. Hickok

Prayer puts God's work in his hands—
and keeps it there.
                              —E.M. Bounds

O Lord, you know what is best for me.
Let this or that be done, as you please.
Give what you will, how much you will,
and when you will.
                              —Thomas a'Kempis

We lie to God in prayer if we do not rely
on him afterwards.
                              —Robert Leighton

The only prayer which a well-meaning
man can pray is, O ye gods, give me
whatever is fitting unto me!
                    —Appollonius of Tyana

What a friend we have in Jesus,
All our sins and griefs to bear!
What a privilege to carry
Everything to God in prayer!

Have we trials and temptations?
Is there trouble anywhere?
We should never be discouraged,
Take it to the Lord in prayer.

Are we weak and heavy laden,
Cumbered with a load of care?
Precious Savior, still our refuge,
Take it to the Lord in prayer.

O what peace we often forfeit,
O what needless pain we bear,
All because we do not carry
Everything to God in prayer!
                    —Joseph Scriven

Take my will, and make it Thine,
It shall be no longer mine;
Take my heart, it is Thine own;
It shall be Thy royal throne.
—Frances Ridley Havergal

Prayer covers the whole of man's life.
There is no thought, feeling, yearning, or
desire, however low, trifling, or vulgar we
may deem it, which if it affects our real
interest or happiness, we may not lay
before God and be sure of sympathy. His
nature is such that our often coming
does not tire him. The whole burden of
the whole life of every man may be rolled
on to God and not weary him, though it
has wearied man.
—Henry Ward Beecher

And since He bids me seek His face,
Believe His word and trust His grace,
I'll cast on Him my every care,
And wait for thee, sweet hour of prayer.
—W.W. Walford

Casting all your care upon Him; for he careth for you.

—1 Pt. 5:7

Cast thy burden upon the Lord, and he shall sustain thee.

—Ps. 55:22

Do not strive in your own strength; cast yourself at the feet of the Lord Jesus, and wait upon Him in the sure confidence that He is with you, and works in you. Strive in prayer; let faith fill your heart— so will you be strong in the Lord, and in the power of His might.

—Andrew Murray

God tells us to burden him with whatever burdens us.

—Anon.

Do what you can and pray for what you cannot yet do.

—Saint Augustine

This is what I found out about religion:
It gives you courage to make decisions
you must make in a crisis, and then the
confidence to leave the result to a Higher
Power. Only by trust in God can a man
carrying responsibility find repose.

—Dwight D. Eisenhower

Always look for ways to act upon the
faith you display in your prayers.

—Anon.

A humble and contrite heart knows that
it can merit nothing before God, and
that all that is necessary is to be recon-
ciled to one's helplessness and let our
holy and almighty God care for us, just
as an infant surrenders himself to his
mother's care.

—O. Hallesby

Before we can pray, "Lord, Thy Kingdom
come," we must be willing to pray, "My
Kingdom go."

—Alan Redpath

Prayer and Forgiveness

No prayers can be heard which do not come from a forgiving heart.

—J.C. Ryle

I firmly believe a great many prayers are not answered because we are not willing to forgive someone.

—Dwight L. Moody

When you pray for anyone, you tend to modify your attitude toward him.

—Norman Vincent Peale

When my children do wrong, I ache to hear their stumbling requests for forgiveness. I'm sure our heavenly Father aches even more deeply to hear from us.

—Anon.

There is nothing that makes us love a man so much as praying for him.

—William Law

WE MUST PRAY, BUT WE MUST ALSO WORK, AND HELP OURSELVES

Ask God's blessing on your work, but don't ask him to do it for you.

—Dame Flora Robson

Prayer indeed is good, but while calling on the gods, a man should himself lend a hand.

—Hippocrates

Prayer, among sane people, has never superseded practical efforts to secure the desired end.

—George Santayana

It is vain to expect our prayers to be heard if we do not strive as well as pray.

—Aesop

He who labors as he prays lifts his heart to God with his hands.

—Bernard of Clairvaux

Pray as if everything depended on God, and work as if everything depended upon man.
—Archbishop Francis J. Spellman

Work as if everything depended upon work and pray as if everything depended upon prayer.
—William Booth

Help yourself and heaven will help you.
—Jean de La Fontaine

Work as if you were to live one hundred years; pray as if you were to die tomorrow.
—Benjamin Franklin

God helps those who help themselves.
—German proverb

God help those who do not help themselves.
—Wilson Mizner

God gives the nuts, but he does not
crack them.

—German proverb

God gives every bird its food, but he
does not throw it into the nest.

—Josiah Holland

It is vain to ask of the gods what man is
capable of supplying for himself.

—Epicurus

Pray devoutly, but hammer stoutly.

—Sir William Gurney Benham

The Ancient Mariner said to Neptune
during a great storm, "O God, you will
save me if you wish, but I am going to
go on holding my tiller straight."

—Michel de Montaigne

Pray to God, but keep rowing to shore.

—Russian proverb

Trust in Allah, but tie your camel first.
                              —Arabic proverb

Call on God, but row away from the
rocks.
                              —Indian proverb

To the man who himself strives earnestly,
God also lends a helping hand.
                              —Aeschylus

Heaven ne'er helps the men who will not
act.
                              —Sophocles

To give pleasure to a single heart by a
single kind act is better than a thousand
head-bowings in prayer.
                              —Sa'Di

You can do more than pray after you
have prayed, but you cannot do more
than pray until you have prayed.
                              —A.J. Gordon

There is a time for all things; a time to preach and a time to pray, but those times have passed away; there is a time to fight, and that time has come!

—General Peter Muhlenberg

To what extent is any given man morally responsible for any given act? We do not know.

—Dr. Alexis Carrel

Prayer is often a temptation to bank on a miracle of God instead of on a moral issue, i.e., it is much easier to ask God to do my work than it is to do it myself. Until we are disciplined properly, we will always be inclined to bank on God's miracles and refuse to do the moral thing ourselves. It is our job, and it will never be done unless we do it.

—Oswald Chambers

SOME RESPONSES TO, AND REWARDS OF, PRAYING

Some people think that prayer just means asking for things, and if they fail to receive exactly what they asked for, they think the whole thing is a fraud.

—Gerald Vann

Real prayer seeks an audience and an answer.

—William S. Plumer

There are three answers to prayer: yes, no, and wait awhile. It must be recognized that no is an answer.

—Ruth Stafford Peale

There are four ways God answers prayer: No, not yet; No, I love you too much; Yes, I thought you'd never ask; Yes, and here's more.

—Anne Lewis

No answer to prayer is an indication of our merit; every answer to prayer is an indication of God's mercy.

—John Blanchard

God answers all true prayer, either in kind or in kindness.

—Adoniram Judson

God is not a cosmic bellboy for whom we can press a button to get things.

—Harry Emerson Fosdick

More things are wrought by prayer than this world dreams of.

—Alfred, Lord Tennyson

When I have a problem I pray about it, and what comes to mind and stays there I assume to be my answer. And this has been right so often that I know it is God's answer.

—J.L. Kraft

Our understanding of God is the answer to prayer; getting things from God is God's indulgence of us. When God stops giving us things, He brings us into the place where we can begin to understand Him.

—Oswald Chambers

When I pray, coincidences happen, and when I don't, they don't.

—William Temple

Who rises from prayer a better man, his prayer is answered.

—George Meredith

My prayers, my God, flow from what I am not; I think Thy answers make me what I am.

—George MacDonald

The great tragedy of life is not unanswered prayer, but unoffered prayer.

—F.B. Meyer

We ought not to tolerate for a minute
the ghastly and grievous thought that
God will not answer prayer.

—Charles Haddon Spurgeon

I tremble for my country when I reflect
that God is just.

—Thomas Jefferson

The answer of our prayers is secured by
the fact that in rejecting them God
would in a certain sense deny His own
nature.

—John Calvin

God answers prayer with certainty. Wish
fulfillment is something else.

—Anon.

God has editing rights over our prayers.
He will ... edit them, correct them, bring
them in line with His will and then hand
them back to us to be resubmitted.

—Stephen Crotts

The greatest blessing of prayer is not
receiving the answer, but being the kind
of person God can trust with His answer.
                                    —Anon.

God delays, but doesn't forget.
                          —Spanish proverb

Beyond our utmost wants
His love and power can bless;
To praying souls he always grants
More than they can express.
                          —John Newton

A generous prayer is never presented in
vain; the petition may be refused, but the
petitioner is always, I believe, rewarded
by some gracious visitation.
                    —Robert Louis Stevenson

Though I am weak, yet God, when
prayed,
Cannot withhold his conquering aid.
                    —Ralph Waldo Emerson

Never was a faithful prayer lost. Some prayers have a longer voyage than others, but then they return with their richer lading at last, so that the praying soul is a gainer by waiting for an answer.

—William Gurnall

I know not by what methods rare,
But this I know: God answers prayer.
I know not if the blessing sought
Will come in just the guise I thought.
I leave my prayer to Him alone
Whose will is wiser than my own.

—Eliza M. Hickok

If we be empty and poor, it is not because God's hand is straitened, but ours is not opened.

—Thomas Manton

I firmly believe a great many prayers are not answered because we are not willing to forgive someone.

—Dwight L. Moody

Our prayers are often filled with selfish "wants"; God always answers with what we need.

—Anon.

The firmament of the Bible is ablaze with answers to prayer.

—T.L. Cuyler

There are two main pitfalls on the road to mastery of the art of prayer. If a person gets what he asks for, his humility is in danger. If he fails to get what he asks for, he is apt to lose confidence. Indeed, no matter whether prayer seems to be succeeding or failing, humility and confidence are two virtues which are absolutely essential.

—A Trappist Monk

Whatever things ye desire, when ye pray, believe that you receive them, and ye shall have them.

—Mk. 11:24

Our prayers run along one road and
God's answers by another, and by and by
they meet.

—Adoniram Judson

Answered prayers cover the field of provi-
dential history as flowers cover western
prairies.

—T.L. Cuyler

Sometimes ... God answers our prayers in
the way our parents do, who reply to the
pleas of their children with "Not just
now" or "I'll have to think about that for
a little while."

—Roy M. Pearson

Asking for anything is allowed with the
understanding that God's answers come
from God's perspective. They are not
always in harmony with our expectations,
for only He knows the whole story.

—Anon.

The king shall joy in thy strength, O
Lord; and in thy salvation how greatly
shall he rejoice! Thou hast given him his
heart's desire, and hast not withheld the
request of his lips.

—Ps. 21:1–2

In seasons of distress and grief,
My soul has often found relief,
And oft escaped the tempter's snare,
By thy return, sweet hour of prayer.

—W.W. Walford

Just when I need Him, He is my all,
Answering when upon Him I call;
Tenderly watching lest I should fall.

—William Poole

May the Lord answer you when you are
in distress; May the name of the God of
Jacob protect you, May he send you help
from the sanctuary and grant you support from Zion.

—Psalms

God answers sharp and sudden on some
    prayers,
And thrusts the thing we have prayed for
    in our face.
A gauntlet with a gift in't.
                    —Elizabeth Barrett Browning

In Gethsemane the holiest of all petition-
ers prayed three times that a certain cup
might pass from Him. It did not. After
that the idea that prayer is recommended
to us as a sort of infallible gimmick may
be dismissed.
                    —C.S. Lewis

Those who trade with heaven by prayer
grow rich by quick returns.
                    —William S. Plumer

The great thing in prayer is to feel that
we are putting our supplications into the
bosom of omnipotent love.
                    —Andrew Murray

We impoverish God in our minds when we say there must be answers to our prayers on the material plane; the biggest answers to our prayers are in the realm of the unseen.

—Oswald Chambers

God's chief gift to those who seek him is Himself.

—E.B. Pusey

Prayer opens our eyes that we may see ourselves and others as God sees us.

—Clara Palmer

The essence of prayer, even of a mystical experience, is the way we are altered to see everything from its life-filled dimension.

—Matthew Fox

Amazing things start happening when we start praying!

—Anon.

If a door slams shut it means that God is
pointing to an open door further on
down.

—Anna Delaney Peale

Prayer enlarges the heart until it is capable of containing God's gift of Himself.

—Mother Teresa

When you go to your knees, God will
help you stand up to anything.

—Anon.

It is impossible to lose your footing while
on your knees.

—Anon.

The influence of prayer on the human
mind and body ... can be measured in
terms of increased physical buoyancy,
greater intellectual vigor, moral stamina,
and a deeper understanding of the realities underlying human relationships.

—Dr. Alexis Carrel

Prayer has marked the trees across the wilderness of a skeptical world to direct the traveler in distress, and all paths lead to a single light.

—Douglas Meador

The man who prays grows, and the muscles of the soul swell from this whipcord to iron bands.

—F.B. Meyer

The exercise of prayer, in those who habitually exert it, must be regarded by us doctors as the most adequate and normal of all the pacifiers of the mind and calmers of the nerves.

—William James

God is a rich and bountiful Father, and He does not forget His children, nor withhold from them anything which it would be to their advantage to receive.

—J.K. Maclean

God's willingness to answer our prayers exceeds our willingness to give good and necessary things to our children, just as far as God's ability, goodness and perfection exceed our infirmities and evil.

—E.M. Bounds

Prayer brings a good spirit in our homes. For God hears prayer. Heaven itself would come down to our homes. And even though we who constitute the home all have our imperfections and our failings, our home would, through God's answer to prayer, become a little paradise.

—O. Hallesby

To thank thee for these gifts of Thine,
For summer's sunshine, winter's snow,
For hearts that kindle, thoughts that
    glow;
But when shall I attain to this—
To thank Thee for the things I miss?

—Thomas Wentworth Higginson

The potency of prayer hath subdued the strength of fire; it hath bridled the rage of lions, hushed anarchy to rest, extinguished wars, appeased the elements, expelled demons, burst the chains of death, expanded the gates of heaven, assuaged diseases, repelled frauds, rescued cities from destruction, stayed the sun in its course, and arrested the progress of the thunderbolt.

—Saint John Chrysostom

God gave you a gift of 86,400 seconds today. Have you used one to say "thank you"?

—William A. Ward

Just as an earthly father knows what is best for his children's welfare, so does God take into consideration the particular needs of His human family, and meets them out of His wonderful storehouse.

—J.K. Maclean

It's Often a Blessing That We Don't Get What We Pray for

More tears are shed over answered prayers than unanswered ones.
— Saint Teresa of Avila

We, ignorant of ourselves, beg often our own harms, which the wise powers deny us for our good.
— William Shakespeare

True prayer always receives what it asks for — or something better.
— Bryon Edwards

Be thankful that God's answers are wiser than your answers.
— William Culbertson

God punishes us mildly by ignoring our prayers, and severely by answering them.
— Richard J. Needham

160

When the gods wish to punish us, they
answer our prayers.

—Oscar Wilde

When the gods are angry with a man,
they give him what he asks for.

—Greek proverb

God alone fully understands what each
one of us needs; we make mistakes continually and pray for things which would
be harmful to us if we received them.
Afterwards we see our mistakes and realize that God is good and wise in not giving us these things, even though we
plead ever so earnestly for them.

—O. Hallesby

I have lived to thank God that all my
prayers have not been answered.

—Jean Ingelow

PRAYER AND FAITH

Prayer is the supreme activity of all that is noblest in our personality, and the essential nature of prayer is faith.

—Oswald Chambers

Teach me, O God, not to torture myself, not to make a martyr out of myself through stifling reflection, but rather teach me to breathe deeply in faith.

—Søren Kierkegaard

Prayer is the voice of faith.

—Horne

The prayer that is faithless is fruitless.

—Thomas Watson

A saint is to put forth his faith in prayer, and afterwards follow his prayer with faith.

—Vavasor Powell

The prayer of faith is the only power in the universe to which the great Jehovah yields.

—Robert Hall

Prayers are heard in heaven very much in proportion to your faith. Little faith will get very great mercies, but great faith still greater.

—Charles Haddon Spurgeon

The beginning of anxiety is the end of faith, and the beginning of true faith is the end of anxiety.

—George Mueller

Faith is the fountain of prayer, and prayer should be nothing else but faith exercised.

—Thomas Manton

Without faith it is impossible to please God, for he that cometh to God must believe that He is.

—Heb. 11:6

Connecting to God
through Prayer

Jesus Christ is a God whom we approach
without pride, and before whom we
humble ourselves without despair.
—Blaise Pascal

When we pray we link ourselves with an
inexhaustible motive power.
—Dr. Alexis Carrel

It is in recognizing the actual presence of
God that we find prayer no longer a
chore, but a supreme delight.
—Gordon Lindsay

Essentially prayer is based on a relationship. We don't converse freely with someone we don't know. We bare our souls
and disclose our hidden secrets only to
someone we trust.
—Dean Register

I who still pray at morning and at eve
Thrice in my life perhaps have truly
    prayed,
Thrice stirred below conscious self
Have felt that perfect disenthrallment
    which is God.

—James Russell Lowell

Prayer is the simplest form of speech
That infant lips can try;
Prayer the sublimest strains that reach
The Majesty on high.

—James Montgomery

Because God is the living God, he can
hear; because he is a loving God, he will
hear; because he is our covenant God, he
has bound himself to hear.

—Charles Haddon Spurgeon

A person must recognize his need for
God before he can request divine aid and
give God due thanks.

—Anon.

MEDITATION

Prayer is when you talk to God; meditation is when you listen to God.

—Diana Robinson

The very best and utmost of attainment in this life is to remain still and let God act and speak in thee.

—Meister Eckhart

You are used to listening to the buzz of the world, but now is the time to develop the inner ear that listens to the inner world. It is time to have a foot in each world, and it can be done.

—Saint Bartholomew

When one devotes oneself to meditation, mental burdens, unnecessary worries, and wandering thoughts drop off one by one; life seems to run smoothly and pleasantly.

—Nyogen Senzaki

But first of all we shall want sunlight;
nothing much can grow in the dark.
Meditation is our step out into the sun.
                                    —*As Bill Sees It*

We must hear Jesus speak if we expect
him to hear us speak.
                          —Charles Haddon Spurgeon

Meditation is a mental discipline that
enables us to do one thing at a time.
                                    —Max Picard

Those who are free of resentful thoughts
surely find peace.
                                    —Buddha

All the troubles of life come upon us
because we refuse to sit quietly for awhile
each day in our rooms.
                                    —Blaise Pascal

OTHER DEFINITIONS OF PRAYER

Prayer is man's greatest means of trapping the infinite resources of God.

—J. Edgar Hoover

Prayer is the heavenly telephone that brings the distant near, till heaven to earth comes down.

—A.B. Simpson

Prayer is conversation with God.

—Clement of Alexandria

Prayer is invoking the impossible.

—Jack W. Hayford

Prayer requires more of the heart than of the tongue.

—Adam Clarke

Prayer is the golden key that opens heaven.

—Thomas Watson

Prayer is the key that opens the door to all that is good in life.

—Anon.

Prayer is a sincere, sensible, affectionate pouring out of the soul to God, through Christ, in the strength and assistance of the Spirit, for such things as God has promised.

—John Bunyan

Prayer is and remains always a native and deepest impulse of the soul of man.

—Thomas Carlyle

Prayer is a strong wall and fortress of the church; it is a goodly Christian's weapon.

—Martin Luther

Prayer is essentially man standing before his God in wonder, awe, and humility; man, made in the image of God, responding to his maker.

—George Appleton

Prayer is the language of a man burdened
with a sense of need.

—E.M. Bounds

Prayer is the incense of a holy heart
Rising to God from bruised and broken
   things,
When kindled by the Spirit's burning
   breath
And upward borne by faith's ascending
   wings.

—A.B. Simpson

For prayer is not a ritual; it is the soul's
inherent response to a relationship with a
loving Father.

—Colleen Townsend Evans

Prayer is the sovereign remedy.

—Robert Hall

Prayer, even more than sheer thought, is
the firmest anchor.

—Jeremiah A. Denton, Jr.

Prayer is our humble answer to the inconceivable surprise of living.

—Abraham Heschel

Prayer is not conquering God's reluctance, but taking hold of God's willingness.

—Phillips Brooks

Prayers are the leeches of care.

—Anon.

Prayer is the soul's breathing itself into the bosom of its heavenly Father.

—Thomas Watson

Prayer is a shield to the soul, a sacrifice to God, and a scourge for Satan.

—John Bunyan

Prayer is the spiritual gymnasium in which we exercise and practice godliness.

—V.L. Crawford

Prayer is exhaling the spirit of man and inhaling the spirit of God.

—Edwin Keith

Prayer means that we have come boldly into the throne room and we are standing in His presence.

—E. W. Kenyon

Prayer is the spirit speaking truth to Truth.

—Philip James Bailey

Prayer is communion with God, usually comprising petition, adoration, praise, confession, and thanksgiving.

—*International Standard Bible Encyclopedia*

Prayer is a rising up and a drawing near to God in mind and in heart, and in spirit.

—Alexander Whyte

Prayer should be the means by which I, at all times, receive all that I need, and, for this reason, be my daily refuge, my daily consolation, my daily joy, my source of rich and inexhaustible joy in life.

—Saint John Chrysostom

Prayer serves as an edge and border to preserve the web of life from unraveling.

—Robert Hall

Prayer does not mean simply to pour out one's heart. It means rather to find the way to God and to speak with him, whether the heart is full or empty.

—Dietrich Bonhoeffer

Prayer is the acid test of devotion.

—Samuel Chadwick

Prayer is the pillow of religion.

—Arab proverb

To labor is to pray.
      —Motto of the Benedictine Order

Prayer is the contemplation of the facts
of life from the highest point of view.
      —Ralph Waldo Emerson

Prayer is our most formidable weapon,
the thing which makes all else we do effi-
cient.
      —E.M. Bounds

Prayer is a cry of distress, a demand for
help, a hymn of love.
      —Dr. Alexis Carrel

Prayer, in its simplest definition, is
merely a wish turned God-ward.
      —Phillips Brooks

Prayer is God's answer to our poverty,
not a power we exercise to obtain an
answer.
      —Oswald Chambers

GENERAL QUOTATIONS
ABOUT PRAYER

The prayers of the Christian are secret,
but their effect cannot be hidden.
—Howard Chandler Robbins

I find in the Psalms much the same range
of mood and expression as I perceive
within my own life of prayer.
—Malcolm Boyd

What I dislike least in my former self are
the moments of prayer.
—André Gide

Revival fires flame where hearts are praying.
—Dick Eastman

Man is the only creature which rises by
bowing, for he finds elevation in his sub-
jection to his Maker.
—Anon.

Our rages, daughters of despair, creep
and squirm like worms. Prayer is the
only form of revolt which remains
upright.

— Georges Bernanos

Prayer reaches out in love to a dying
world and says, "I care."

— Dick Eastman

Lord, till I reach that blissful shore,
No privilege so dear shall be
As thus my inmost soul to pour
In prayer to thee.

— Charlotte Elliott

Prayer is an all-efficient panoply, a treasure undiminished, a mine which is
never exhausted, a sky unobscured by
clouds, a heaven unruffled by the storm.
It is the root, the fountain, the mother of
a thousand blessings.

— Saint John Chrystostom

To pray together, in whatever tongue or ritual, is the most tender brotherhood of hope and sympathy that man can contract in this life.

—Anne Germain De Stael

The deepest wishes of the heart find expression in secret prayer.

—George E. Rees

We are never more like Christ than in prayers of intercession.

—Austin Phelps

The spirit of prayer is the fruit and token of the Spirit of adoption.

—John Newton

I am used to praying when I am alone, thank God. But when I come together with other people, when I need more than ever to pray, I still cannot get used to it.

—Leo Tolstoy

I would rather stand against the cannons
of the wicked than against the prayers of
the righteous.

—Thomas Lye

Restraining prayer, we cease to fight;
Prayer keeps the Christian's armor bright;
And Satan trembles when he sees
The weakest saint upon his knees.

—William Cowper

Nothing is discussed more and practiced
less than prayer.

—Anon.

God dwells where we let God in.

—Menachem Mendel

I always love to begin a journey on
Sundays, because I shall have the prayers
of the church to preserve all that travel
by land, or by water.

—Jonathan Swift

Courage is not afraid to weep, and she is not afraid to pray, even when she is not sure who she is praying to.

—J. Ruth Gendler

God warms his hands at man's heart when he prays.

—Masefield

Turn your doubts to question; turn your question to prayers; turn your prayers to God.

—Mark R. Litteton

In the calm of sweet communion
Let thy daily work be done;
In the peace of soul-outpouring
Care be banished, patience won;
And if earth with its enchantments
Seek thy spirit to enthrall,
Ere thou listen, ere thou answer,
Turn to Jesus, tell Him all.

—G.M. Taylor

Nor it is an objection to say that we must understand a prayer if it is to have its true effect. That simply is not the case. Who understands the wisdom of a flower? Yet we can take pleasure in it.
—Rudolph Steiner

Saints of the early church reaped great harvests in the field of prayer and found the mercy seat to be a mine of untold treasures.
—Charles Haddon Spurgeon

The wings of prayer carry high and far.
—Anon.

Prayer, like radium, is a luminous and self-generating form of energy.
—Dr. Alexis Carrel

Whatever you do in revenge against your brother will appear all at once in your heart at the time of payer.
—The Desert Fathers

Any concern too small to be turned into
a prayer is too small to be made into a
burden.

—Corrie ten Boom

Never say you will pray about a thing;
pray about it.

—Oswald Chambers

If we ask anything according to his will,
he heareth us.

—1 Jn. 5:14

Show me your ways, O Lord, teach me
your paths; guide me in your truth and
teach me, for you are God my Savior,
and my hope is in you all day long.

—Psalms

Doubt not but God who sits on high,
Thy secret prayers can hear;
When a dead wall thus cunningly
Conveys soft whispers to the ear.

—Anon.

The granting of prayer, when offered in the name of Jesus, reveals the Father's love to him, and the honor which he has put upon him.

—Charles Haddon Spurgeon

Our praying, to be strong, must be buttressed by holy living. The life of faith perfects the prayer of faith.

—E.M. Bounds

A Chinese Christian prayed every day ... "Lord, reform Thy world, beginning with me."

—Franklin Delano Roosevelt

Create in me a clean heart, O God.

—Ps. 51:10

PART FOUR

FORGIVENESS

FORGIVING AND FORGETTING— REALLY LETTING GO

The stupid neither forgive nor forget; the naive forgive and forget; the wise forgive, but do not forget.

—Thomas Szasz

Once a woman has forgiven a man, she must not reheat his sins for breakfast.

—Marlene Dietrich

Keeping score of old scores and scars, getting even and one-upping, always make you less than you are.

—Malcolm Forbes

"I can forgive, but I cannot forget" is only another way of saying, "I will not forgive." Forgiveness ought to be like a canceled note—torn in two and burned up so that it never can be shown against one.

—Henry Ward Beecher

Forgiveness means letting go of the past.
　　　　　　　　　　　—Gerald Jampolsky

The secret of forgiving everything is to
understand nothing.
　　　　　　　　　　　—George Bernard Shaw

Nobody ever forgets where he buried a
hatchet.
　　　　　　　　　　　—Kin Hubbard

There's no point in burying a hatchet if
you're going to put up a marker on the
site.
　　　　　　　　　　　—Sydney Harris

Not the power to remember, but its very
opposite, the power to forget, is a necessary condition for our existence.
　　　　　　　　　　　—Sholem Asch

To be wronged is nothing unless you
continue to remember it.
　　　　　　　　　　　—Confucius

Only the Strong Can Forgive

The weak can never forgive. Forgiveness
is the attribute of the strong.
> —Mahatma Ghandi

Only the brave know how to forgive.... A
coward never forgave; it is not in his
nature.
> —Laurence Sterne

Any man can seek revenge; it takes a king
or prince to grant a pardon.
> —Arthur J. Rehrat

To be angry about trifles is mean and
childish; to rage and be furious is
brutish; and to maintain perpetual wrath
is akin to the practice and temper of dev-
ils; but to prevent and suppress rising
resentment is wise and glorious, is manly
and divine.
> —Isaac Watts

RESENTMENTS, HATRED, AND ANGER

Resentment is the "number one" offender. It destroys more alcoholics than anything else. From it stem all forms of spiritual disease, for we have been not only mentally and physically ill, we have been spiritually sick.

—Alcoholics Anonymous

Hate would destroy him who hated.

—Louis L'Amour

Hate is a prolonged form of suicide.

—Douglas V. Steere

To carry a grudge is like being stung to death by one bee.

—William H. Walton

Resentments are burdens we don't need to carry.

—Anon.

Anger as soon as fed is dead, 'tis starving makes it fat.

—Emily Dickinson

Anger dwells only in the bosom of fools.

—Albert Einstein

Without forgiveness life is governed ... by an endless cycle of resentment and retaliation.

—Robert Assaglioli

Bitterness imprisons life; love releases it.

—Harry Emerson Fosdick

If the will remains in protest, it stays dependent on that which it is protesting against.

—Rollo May

If you hate a person, you hate something in him that is part of yourself.

—Herman Hesse

Whom they have injured, they also hate.
—Marcus Annaeus Seneca

Anger is a short madness.

—Horace

The angry people are those people who
are most afraid.
—Dr. Robert Anthony

Holding on to anger is like grasping a
hot coal with the intent of throwing it
at someone else; you are the one who
gets burned.

—Buddha

Anger is a killing thing: it kills the man
who angers, for each rage leaves him less
than he had been before—it takes something from him.

—Louis L'Amour

FORGIVENESS, LOVE, AND GOD

One forgives to the degree that one loves.
—Francois de La Rochefoucauld

We never ask God to forgive anybody
except when we haven't.
—Elbert Hubbard

Forgiveness is God's command.
—Martin Luther

God will forgive me the foolish remarks I
have made about Him just as I will forgive my opponents the foolish things
they have written about me, even though
they are spiritually as inferior to me as I
to thee, O God!
—Heinrich Heine

One is as one is, and the love that can't
encompass both is a poor sort of love.
—Marya Mannes

God will forgive me, that is His business.
—Heinrich Heine

Forgiveness is the final form of love.
—Reinhold Niebuhr

Love is an act of endless forgiveness, a tender look which becomes a habit.
—Peter Ustinov

Today I forgive all those who have ever offended me. I give my love to all thirsty hearts, both to those who love me and to those who do not love me.
—Paramahansa Yogananda

Let all bitterness, and wrath, and anger, and clamour, and evil speaking, be put away from you, with all malice; and be ye kind to one another, tenderhearted, forgiving one another, even as God, for Christ's sake, hath forgiven you.
—Eph. 4:31–32

HOW FORGIVENESS HELPS US

Forgiveness is the answer to the child's dream of a miracle by which what is broken is made whole again, what is soiled is again made clean.

—Dag Hammarskjold

To forgive is the highest, most beautiful form of love. In return, you will receive untold peace and happiness.

—Robert Muller

Forgiveness is the key to action and freedom.

—Hannah Arendt

Forgiveness is all-powerful. Forgive-ness heals all ills.

—Catherine Ponder

I can have peace of mind only when I forgive rather than judge.

—Gerald Jampolsky

The forgiving state of mind is a magnetic
power for attracting good.
                              —Catherine Ponder

Judge not, that ye be not judged.
                              —Mt. 7:1

It is in pardoning that we are pardoned.
                              —Saint Francis of Assisi

Forgiveness is the way to true health and
happiness.
                              —Gerald Jampolsky

Humanity is never so beautiful as when
praying for forgiveness, or else forgiving
another.
                              —Jean Paul Richter

Forgiveness is the remission of sins. For it
is by this that what has been lost, and
was found, is saved from being lost again.
                              —Saint Augustine

WE MUST FORGIVE OURSELVES, TOO

I can pardon everybody's mistakes except
my own.
—Marcus Cato the Elder

If you haven't forgiven yourself something, how can you forgive others?
—Dolores Huerta

How unhappy is he who cannot forgive
himself.
—Publilius Syrus

The moment an individual can accept
and forgive himself, even a little, is the
moment in which he becomes to some
degree lovable.
—Eugene Kennedy

They may not deserve forgiveness, but I
do.
—Anon.

I forgive myself for having believed for so long that ... I was never good enough to have, get, be what I wanted.

—Ceanne DeRohan

Be grateful for yourself ... be thankful.

—William Saroyan

Every man treats himself as society treats the criminal.

—Harvey Fergusson

To understand is to forgive, even oneself.

—Alexander Chase

Give us this day our daily bread.
And forgive us our debts,
as we forgive our debtors.

—Mt. 6:11–12

He that cannot forgive others breaks the bridge over which he must pass himself; for every man has need to be forgiven.

—Thomas Fuller

FORGIVENESS DOESN'T ALWAYS PLEASE THOSE WE FORGIVE

Always forgive your enemies; nothing annoys them so much.

—Oscar Wilde

Forgiveness is the noblest vengeance.

—H.G. Bohn

There is no revenge so complete as forgiveness.

—Josh Billings

It is easier to forgive an enemy than a friend.

—Madame Dorothee Deluzy

Many promising reconciliations have broken down because while both parties came prepared to forgive, neither party came prepared to be forgiven.

—Charles William

General Quotations
about Forgiveness

Forgiveness is man's deepest need and highest achievement.

—Horace Bushnell

Abandon your animosities and make your sons Americans!

—Robert E. Lee

Her breasts and arms ached with the beauty of her own forgiveness.

—Meridel Le Sueur

Dream of your brother's kindnesses instead of dwelling in your dreams on his mistakes. Select his thoughtfulness to dream about instead of counting up the hurts he gave.

—*A Course In Miracles*

Life is an adventure in forgiveness.

—Norman Cousins

Forgiveness is the highest and most difficult of all moral lessons.

—Joseph Jacobs

The cut worm forgives the plow.

—William Blake

The fragrance of the violet sheds on the heel that has crushed it.

—Mark Twain

How shall I love the sin, yet keep the sense,
And love the offender, yet detest the offence?

—Alexander Pope

Forgiveness is the giving, and so the receiving, of life.

—George Macdonald

Who would care to question the ground of forgiveness or compassion?

—Joseph Conrad

When you pray for anyone you tend to
modify your personal attitude toward
him.
                    —Norman Vincent Peale

O friends, I pray tonight,
Keep not your kisses for my dead cold
    brow.
The way is lonely; let me feel them now.
Think gently of me; I am travel-worn,
My faltering feet are pierced with many a
    thorn.
Forgive! O hearts estranged, forgive, I
    plead!
When ceaseless bliss is mine I shall not
    need
The tenderness for which I long tonight.
                    —Belle Eugenia Smith

Let us forget and forgive injuries.
                    —Miguel de Cervantes

Even a stopped clock is right twice a day.
                    —Marie von Ebner-Eschenbach

It is very easy to forgive others their mistakes; it takes more grit and gumption to forgive them for having witnessed your own.

—Jessamyn West

Forgiving means to pardon the unpardonable, faith means believing the unbelievable, and hoping means to hope when things are hopeless.

—G.K. Chesterton

To err is human; to forgive, divine.

—Alexander Pope

PART FIVE

COUNTING OUR BLESSINGS

We Should Be Aware of the Blessings of Our Everyday Lives

Yes, there is a Nirvanah: it is in leading your sheep to a green pasture, and in putting your child to sleep, and in writing the last line of your poem.

—Kahlil Gibran

That daily life is really good one appreciates when one wakes from a horrible dream, or when one takes the first outing after a sickness. Why not realize it now?

—William Lyon Phelps

When I first open my eyes upon the morning meadows and look out upon the beautiful world, I thank God I am alive.

—Ralph Waldo Emerson

There is nothing so bitter that a patient mind cannot find some solace for it.

—Marcus Annaeus Seneca

The unthankful heart ... discovers no mercies; but let the thankful heart sweep through the day and, as the magnet finds the iron, so it will find, in every hour, some heavenly blessings!

—Henry Ward Beecher

Each day comes bearing its own gifts. Untie the ribbons.

—Ruth Ann Schabacker

Be on the lookout for mercies. The more we look for them, the more of them we will see.... Better to loose count while naming your blessings than to lose your blessings to counting your troubles.

—Maltbie D. Babcock

Good heavens, of what uncostly material is our earthly happiness composed ... if we only knew it. What incomes have we not had from a flower, and how unfailing are the dividends of the seasons.

—James Russell Lowell

The man who thinks his wife, his baby,
his house, his horse, his dog, and himself
severely unequalled, is almost sure to be a
good-humored person.

—Oliver Wendell Holmes

I thank You God for this most amazing
day; for the leaping greenly spirits of
trees and a blue true dream of sky; and
for everything which is natural which is
infinite which is yes.

—e.e. cummings

Why do some people always see beautiful
skies and grass and lovely flowers and
incredible human beings, while others are
hard-pressed to find anything or any
place that is beautiful?

—Leo Buscaglia

Most human beings have an almost infinite capacity for taking things for
granted.

—Aldous Huxley

When something does not insist on being noticed, when we aren't grabbed by the collar or struck on the skull by a presence or an event, we take for granted the very things that most deserve our gratitude.

—Cynthia Ozick

Normal day, let me be aware of the treasure you are. Let me learn from you, love you, bless you before you depart. Let me not pass you by in quest of some rare and perfect tomorrow. Let me hold you while I may, for it may not always be so. One day I shall dig my nails into the earth, or bury my face in the pillow, or stretch myself taut, or raise my hands to the sky and want, more than all the world, your return.

—Mary Jean Iron

We are never either so wretched or so happy as we say we are.

—Honore de Balzac

Is life so wretched? Isn't it rather your hands which are too small, your vision which is muddled? You are the one who must grow up.

—Dag Hammarskjold

We can be thankful to a friend for a few acres or a little money; and yet for the freedom and command of the whole earth, and for the great benefits of our being, our life, health, and reason, we look upon ourselves as under no obligation.

—Marcus Annaeus Seneca

The best things are nearest: breath in your nostrils, light in your eyes, flowers at your feet, duties at your hand, the path of God just before you. Then do not grasp at the stars, but do life's plain, common work as it comes, certain that daily duties and daily bread are the sweetest things of life.

—Robert Louis Stevenson

Looking for Silver Linings

Our real blessings often appear to us in the shape of pains, losses and disappointments.

—Joseph Addison

Adversity has the same effect on a man that severe training has on the pugilist: it reduces him to his fighting weight.

—Josh Billings

Most of my major disappointments have turned out to be blessings in disguise. So whenever anything bad does happen to me, I kind of sit back and feel, well, if I give this enough time, it'll turn out that this was good, so I shan't worry about it too much.

—William Gaines

Sometimes the best deals are the ones you don't make.

—Bill Veeck

207

The advantages of a losing team: (1) There is everything to hope for and nothing to fear. (2) Defeats do not disturb one's sleep. (3) An occasional victory is a surprise and a delight. (4) There is no danger of any club passing you. (5) You are not asked fifty times a day, "What was the score?"; people take it for granted that you lost.

—Elmer E. Bates

That which does not kill me makes me stronger.

—Friedrich Nietzsche

Trouble is only opportunity in work clothes.

—Henry J. Kaiser

Not being beautiful was the true blessing.... Not being beautiful forced me to develop my inner resources. The pretty girl has a handicap to overcome.

—Golda Meir

The difficulties, hardships and trials of life, the obstacles ... are positive blessings. They knit the muscles more firmly, and teach self-reliance.

—William Matthews

Many a man curses the rain that falls upon his head, and knows not that it brings abundance to drive away hunger.

—Saint Basil

You will never be the person you can be if pressure, tension and discipline are taken out of your life.

—Dr. James G. Bilkey

God brings men into deep waters not to drown them, but to cleanse them.

—Aughey

Some troubles, like a protested note of a solvent debtor, bear interest.

—Honore de Balzac

Failure changes for the better, success for the worse.
—Marcus Annaeus Seneca

The basis of optimism is sheer terror.
—Oscar Wilde

No evil is without its compensation ... it is not the loss itself, but the estimate of the loss, that troubles us.
—Marcus Annaeus Seneca

Let me embrace thee, sour adversity, for wise men say it is the wisest course.
—William Shakespeare

Give thanks for sorrow that teaches you pity; for pain that teaches you courage—and give exceeding thanks for the mystery which remains a mystery still—the veil that hides you from the infinite, which makes it possible for you to believe in what you cannot see.
—Robert Nathan

LIFE ITSELF IS A BLESSING

There is no wealth but life.
—John Ruskin

Just to be is a blessing. Just to live is holy.
—Abraham Heschel

I like living. I have sometimes been
wildly, despairingly, acutely miserable,
racked with sorrow, but through it all I
still know quite certainly that just to be
alive is a grand thing.
—Agatha Christie

Life is the first gift, love is the second,
and understanding the third.
—Marge Piercy

Be glad of life because it gives you the
chance to love, and to work, and to play
and to look up at the stars.
—Henry Van Dyke

To be alive, to see, to walk ... it's all a miracle. I have adapted the technique of living life from miracle to miracle.

—Arthur Rubinstein

This is another day! Are its eyes blurred
With maudlin grief for any wasted past?
A thousand thousand failures shall not daunt!
Let dust clasp dust, death, death; I am alive!

—Don Marquis

The mere sense of living is joy enough.

—Emily Dickinson

However mean your life is, meet it and live it; do not shun it and call it hard names. It is not so bad as you are. It looks poorest when you are richest. The fault-finder will find faults even in Paradise. Love your life.

—Henry David Thoreau

THE SIMPLEST THINGS
ARE BLESSINGS

Only a stomach that rarely feels hungry
scorns common things.

—Horace

Is it so small a thing to have enjoyed the
sun, to have lived light in the spring, to
have loved, to have thought, to have
done?

—Matthew Arnold

It is strange what a contempt men have
for the joys that are offered them freely.

—Georges Duhamel

Grateful for the blessing lent of simple
tastes and mind content!

—Oliver Wendell Holmes

To have a full stomach and fixed income
are no small things .

—Elbert Hubbard

Most of us miss out on life's big prizes.
The Pulitzer. The Nobel. Oscars. Tonys.
Emmys. But we're all eligible for life's
small pleasures. A pat on the back. A kiss
behind the ear. A four-pound bass. A full
moon. An empty parking space. A crackling fire. A great meal. A glorious sunset.
Hot soup. Cold beer. Don't fret about
copping life's grand awards. Enjoy its tiny
delights. There are plenty for all of us.

—United Technologies
Corporation advertisement

How can they say my life is not a success? Have I not for more than sixty
years gotten enough to eat and escaped
being eaten?

—Logan Pearsall Smith

Sunshine is delicious, rain is refreshing,
wind braces us up, snow is exhilarating;
there is really no such thing as bad
weather, only different kinds of good
weather.

—John Ruskin

You say grace before meals. All right. But I say grace before the concert and the opera, and grace before the play and pantomime, and grace before I open a book, and grace before sketching, painting, swimming, fencing, boxing, walking, playing, dancing and grace before I dip the pen in the ink.

—G.K. Chesterton

Thank God for dirty dishes; they have a
  tale to tell.
While other folks go hungry, we're eating
  pretty well.
With home, and health, and happiness,
  we shouldn't want to fuss;
For by this stack of evidence, God's very
  good to us.

—Anon.

People call me an optimist, but I'm really an appreciator.

—Julian Simon

It Could be Worse

If you can't be thankful for what you receive, be thankful for what you escape.

—Anon.

Even though we can't have all we want, we ought to be thankful we don't get all we deserve.

—Anon.

Happy the man who can count his sufferings.

—Ovid

Happiness is composed of misfortunes avoided.

—Alphonse Karr

Considering the fortune you might have lost, you'll have to admit you're rich already.

—John Rothchild

I thank Thee first because I was never robbed before; second, because although they took my purse they did not take my life; third, because although they took my all, it was not much; and fourth because it was I who was robbed, and not I who robbed.

—Matthew Henry

Think of the ills from which you are exempt.

—Joseph Joubert

A man should always consider ... how much more unhappy he might be than he is.

—Joseph Addison

The happiness of any given life is to be measured not by its joys and pleasures, but by the extent to which it has been free from suffering, from positive evil.

—Arthur Schopenhauer

Better to suffer than to die.
> —Francois de La Fontaine

For grief unsuffered, tears unshed, for
    clouds that scattered overhead;
For pestilence that came not high, for
    dangers great that passed me by;
For sharp suspicion smoothed, allayed,
    for doubt dispelled that made afraid;
For fierce temptation well withstood, for
    evil plot that brought forth good;
For weakened links in friendship's chain
    that, sorely tested, stood the strain;
For harmless blows with malice dealt, for
    base ingratitude unfelt;
For hatred's sharp unuttered word, for
    bitter jest unknown, unheard;
For every evil turned away, unmeasured
    thanks I give today.
> —Anon.

Better a little fire to warm us than a great
one to burn us.
> —Thomas Fuller

WE SHOULD BE THANKFUL FOR WHAT WE'VE GOT

A prudent man will think more important what fate has conceded to him, than what it has denied.

—Baltasar Gracian

He is a man of sense who does not grieve for what he has not, but rejoices in what he has.

—Epictetus

For everything you have missed, you have gained something else.

—Ralph Waldo Emerson

Few love what they may have.

—Ovid

The knowledge that something remains yet unenjoyed impairs our enjoyment of the good before us.

—Samuel Johnson

It is not customary to love what one has.
—Anatole France

When we cannot get what we love, we must love what is within our reach.
—French proverb

Long only for what you have.
—André Gide

Happy thou art not; for what thou hast not, still thou striv'est to get; and what thou hast, forget'est.
—William Shakespeare

Men ... always think that something they are going to get is better than what they have got.
—John Oliver Hobbes

May we never let the things we can't have, or don't have, spoil our enjoyment of the things we do have and can have.
—Richard L. Evans

A man can refrain from wanting what he
has not, and cheerfully make the best of
a bird in the hand.
—Marcus Annaeus Seneca

Take full account of the excellencies
which you possess, and in gratitude
remember how you would hanker after
them, if you had them not.
—Marcus Aurelius

If there is a sin against life, it consists
perhaps not so much in despairing of life
as in hoping for another, and in eluding
the implacable grandeur of this life.
—Albert Camus

Welcome everything that comes to you,
but do not long for anything else.
—André Gide

A wise man cares not for what he cannot
have.
—Anon.

The tulip is, among flowers, what the peacock is among birds. A tulip lacks scent, a peacock has an unpleasant voice. The one takes pride in its garb, the other in its tail.

—French proverb

There is a mortal breed most full of futility. In contempt of what is at hand, they strain into the future, hunting impossibilities on the wings of ineffectual hopes.

—Pindar

What you really value is what you miss, not what you have.

—Jorge Luis Borges

Slight not what is near though aiming at what is far.

—Euripides

Greediness of getting more, deprives ... the enjoyment of what it had got.

—Thomas Sprat

222

WE OFTEN DON'T APPRECIATE
WHAT WE HAVE UNTIL WE LOSE IT

So long as we can lose any happiness, we
possess some.
> —Booth Tarkington

Generally the man with a good wife, or
the woman with a good husband, or the
children with good parents discover too
late the goodness they overlooked while
it was in full bloom.
> —James Douglas

The best things in life are appreciated
most after they have been lost.
> —Roy L. Smith

Happiness always looks small while you
hold it in your hands, but let it go, and
you learn at once how big and precious
it is.
> —Maxim Gorky

We never know the worth of water till
the well is dry.

—English proverb

The way to love anything is to realize
that it may be lost.

—G.K. Chesterton

Eden is that old-fashioned house we
dwell in every day
Without suspecting our abode, until we
drive away.

—Emily Dickinson

Only with a new ruler do you realize the
value of the old.

—Burmese proverb

I remember those happy days and often
wish I could speak into the ears of the
dead the gratitude which was due to
them in life and so ill-returned.

—Gwyn Thomas

GIVING THANKS

Thanksgiving is a sure index of spiritual health.

—Maurice Dametz

A thankful heart is not only the greatest virtue, but the parent of all other virtues.

—Cicero

If the only prayer you say in your whole life is "Thank you," that would suffice.

—Meister Eckhart

Who does not thank for little will not thank for much.

—Estonian proverb

The Pilgrims made seven times more graves than huts. No Americans have been more impoverished than these who, nevertheless, set aside a day of thanksgiving.

—H.U. Westermayer

The greatest saint in the world is not he who prays most or fasts most; it is not he who gives alms, or is most eminent for temperance, chastity or justice. It is he who is most thankful to God.

—William Law

Joy is the simplest form of gratitude.

—Karl Barth

He who receives a benefit with gratitude repays the first installment on his debt.

—Marcus Annaeus Seneca

Not what we say about our blessings, but how we use them, is the true measure of our thanksgiving.

—W.T. Purkiser

The unthankful heart ... discovers no mercies; but the thankful heart ... will find, in every hour, some heavenly blessings.

—Henry Ward Beecher

Happiness is itself a kind of gratitude.
—Joseph Wood Krutch

The beginning of men's rebellion against God was, and is, the lack of a thankful heart.
—Francis Schaeffer

One of life's gifts is that each of us, no matter how tired and downtrodden, finds reasons for thankfulness.
—J. Robert Maskin

We give thanks for unknown blessings already on their way.
—Sacred ritual chant

The private and personal blessings we enjoy—the blessings of immunity, safeguard, liberty and integrity—deserve the thanksgiving of a whole life.
—Jeremy Taylor

Gratitude is the memory of the heart.
—Massieu

What Is Enough?

There is satiety in all things, in sleep, and love-making, in the loveliness of singing and the innocent dance.

—Homer

The average man is rich enough when he has a little more than he has got.

—William Ralph Inge

What is the proper limit for wealth? It is, first, to have what is necessary; and, second, to have what is enough.

—Marcus Annaeus Seneca

He has enough who is contented with little.

—Anon.

Nothing is enough to the man for whom enough is too little.

—Epicurus

Let him who has enough wish for nothing more.

—Horace

Sufficiency's enough for men of sense.
—Euripides

You never know what is enough unless you know what is more than enough.
—William Blake

Enough is as good as a feast.
—John Heywood

A wise man will desire no more than what he may get justly, use soberly, distribute cheerfully, and leave contently.
—Benjamin Franklin

Money and time are the heaviest burdens of life, and the unhappiest of all mortals are those who have more of either than they know how to use.
—Samuel Johnson

Whoever is not in his coffin and the dark grave, let him know he has enough.

—Walt Whitman

This only grant me, that my means may lie too low for envy, for contempt too high.

—Abraham Cowley

Moderation is the key to lasting enjoyment.

—Hosea Ballou

The use we make of our fortune determines as to its sufficiency. A little is enough if used wisely, and too much is not enough if expended foolishly.

—Christian Bovee

Nothing in excess.

—Solon

Ask the gods nothing excessive.

—Aeschylus

GREED

He who is greedy is always in want.

—Horace

To be able to dispense with good things
is tantamount to possessing them.

—Jean Francois Regnard

The hardest thing is to take less when
you can get more.

—Kin Hubbard

Whoever does not regard what he has as
most ample wealth is unhappy, though
he is master of the world.

—Epicurus

No gain satisfies a greedy mind.

—Latin proverb

Greed lessens what is gathered.

—Arab proverb

231

For greed, all nature is too little.
—Marcus Annaeus Seneca

Of all the people in the world, those who want the most are those who have the most.
—David Grayson

Who covets more is evermore a slave.
—Robert Herrick

Greed is a bottomless pit which exhausts the person in an endless effort to satisfy the need without ever reaching satisfaction.
—Erich Fromm

If you desire many things, many things will seem but a few.
—Benjamin Franklin

The heart is great which shows moderation in the midst of prosperity.
—Marcus Annaeus Seneca

Man needs so little ... yet he begins
wanting so much.

>—Louis L'Amour

Man never has what he wants, because
what he wants is everything.

>—C.F. Ramuz

Want is a growing giant whom the coat
of Have was never large enough to cover.

>—Ralph Waldo Emerson

We are no longer happy so soon as we
wish to be happier.

>—Walter Savage Landor

I have learned to seek my happiness by
limiting my desires, rather than in
attempting to satisfy them.

>—John Stuart Mill

How many things there are which I do
not want.

>—Socrates

Were a man to order his life by the rules of true reason, a frugal substance joined to a contented mind is for him great riches.

—Lucretius

One is never fortunate or as unfortunate as one imagines.

—Francois de La Rochefoucauld

If your desires be endless, your cares and fears will be so, too.

—Thomas Fuller

He is not rich that possesses much, but he that covets no more; and he is not poor that enjoys little, but he that wants too much.

—Beaumont

Independence may be found in comparative as well as in absolute abundance; I mean where a person contracts his desires within the limits of his fortune.

—William Shenstone

THERE ARE ALWAYS OTHERS
WORSE OFF THAN US

One never hugs one's good luck so affectionately as when listening to the relation of some horrible misfortunes which has overtaken others.

—Alexander Smith

If you would but exchange places with the other fellow, how much more you could appreciate your own position.

—Victor E. Gardner

We should learn, by reflection on the misfortunes of others, that there is nothing singular in those which befall ourselves.

—Thomas Fitzosborne

Double—no, triple—our troubles and we'd still be better off than any other people on earth.

—Ronald Reagan

BEING THANKFUL FOR
OUR ABILITIES AND TALENTS

I may not amount to much, but at least I am unique.

> —Jean-Jacques Rousseau

Happy is the man who can do only one thing: in doing it, he fulfills his destiny.

> —Joseph Joubert

The real tragedy of life is not being limited to one talent, but in failing to use that one talent.

> —Edgar Watson Howe

Too many people overvalue what they are not and undervalue what they are.

> —Malcolm Forbes

One well-cultivated talent, deepened and enlarged, is worth one hundred shallow faculties.

> —William Matthews

Contentment

Nothing will content him who is not content with a little.

—Greek proverb

Contentment is worth more than riches.

—German proverb

Be content with what thou hast received, and smooth thy frowning forehead.

—Hafez

He is poor who does not feel content.

—Japanese proverb

If thou covetest riches, ask not but for contentment, which is an immense treasure.

—Sa'Di

My crown is called content, a crown that seldom kings enjoy.

—William Shakespeare

It is right to be contented with what we have, never with what we are.

—Mackintosh

Be content with your lot; one cannot be first in everything.

—Aesop

Content may dwell in all stations. To be low, but above contempt, may be high enough to be happy.

—Sir Thomas Browne

True contentment ... is the power of getting out of any situation all that there is in it. It is arduous, and it is rare.

—G.K. Chesterton

Poor and content is rich, and rich enough.

—William Shakespeare

The greatest wealth is contentment with a little.

—Anon.

And be content with such things as ye
have.

—Heb. 13:5

Everything has its wonders, even darkness and silence, and I learn, whatever
state I may be in, therein to be content.

—Helen Keller

Until you make peace with who you are,
you'll never be content with what you
have.

—Doris Mortman

True contentment depends not upon
what we have; a tub was large enough for
Diogenes, but a world was too little for
Alexander.

—Charles Caleb Colton

Try to live the life of the good man who
is more than content with what is allo-
cated to him.

—Marcus Aurelius

HAPPINESS

Happiness is a result of the relative strengths of positive and negative feelings, rather than an absolute amount of one or the other.

—Norman Bradburn

The best way for a person to have happy thoughts is to count his blessings and not his cash.

—Anon.

To be without some of the things you want is an indispensable part of happiness.

—Bertrand Russell

Man is fond of counting his troubles, but he does not count his joys. If he counted them up as he ought to, he would see that every lot has enough happiness provided for it.

—Fyodor Dostoyevsky

You will live wisely if you are happy in your lot.

—Horace

Talk happiness. The world is sad enough without your woe. No path is wholly rough.

—Ella Wheeler Wilcox

I am happy and content because I think I am.

—Alain-Rene Lesage

Unhappy is the man, though he rule the world, who doesn't consider himself supremely blessed.

—Marcus Annaeus Seneca

The happiness which is lacking makes one think even the happiness one has unbearable.

—Joseph Roux

General Quotations about Our Blessings

Life is hard. Next to what?

—Anon.

'Tis better to have loved and lost than never to have loved at all.

—Alfred, Lord Tennyson

No one is satisfied with his fortune, or dissatisfied with his intellect.

—Antoinette Deshouliere

Over a period of time it's been driven home to me that I'm not going to be the most popular writer in the world, so I'm always happy when anything in any way is accepted.

—Stephen Sondheim

In the country of the blind, the one-eyed man is king.

—Michael Apostolius

A man with ambition and love for his blessings here on earth is ever so alive. Having been alive, it won't be so hard in the end to lie down and rest.

—Pearl Bailey

Be satisfied, and pleased with what thou
    art,
Act cheerfully and well thou allotted
    part;
Enjoy the present hour, be thankful for
    the past,
And neither fear, nor wish, the
    approaches of the last.

—Martial